The Magician's Fight!

~How The Magician fought for His Art~

James Charles Bouffard, Psy.D., Ph.D.

(Edited by: Lisa Diane Branscome)

Second Edition*

Includes:
Magical Facts & Secrets, Magical Trivia
and
A Magical Glossary

Illustrated

*Formally published as **The Magician and His Art**.
*As **Dr. Jimini, M.E. [Magical Entertainer]**

Lynn Paulo Foundation
Pomona, California

Copyright © 2008 Dr. James Charles Bouffard
All rights reserved.

No part of this work may be reproduced in any form (including storage in a retrieval system) without written permission of the author. Exceptions are brief quotations embodied in critical articles and reviews.

ISBN 978-0-6151-9358-8

Printed in the United States of America

Other works by Dr. Bouffard:

Be A Private Investigator
A Quest For Absolute Power
The Entrepreneurial Ben Franklin
Defiance! A Saga of David Crockett and the Alamo

Dedicated to the memory of
Earle Lockman,
magician, escape artist
and friend,
who died at the age of 81
while still entertaining us.

Though many years have passed,
I remember clearly
his instructive talks.

Strange we should remember the
words more after the
voice has been stilled.

Preface

Oppositions to the art of magic were formally of a religious essence, devolving from Old Testament mandates to punish by death the sin of witchery. Relatively, severe penalties were borne for practicing magic among the Egyptians, Greeks and Romans.

In 1542, Henry VIII of England forbad conjuration in a royal decree. Twenty-one years later his daughter, Queen Elizabeth I, took up a quill to condemn the magician as a servant of Satan.

During the middle ages, and well into the 18th century, upbraiding of magical entertainers were implemented by witch-hunts and trials.

Although not connected yet unfavorably affected, domininant among the witch-hunters were Increase Mather and his son Cotton, both Boston ministers, who presided notoriously over the Salem witch trials in Massachusetts.

Preface

Witch-hunts, trials and executions were carried out en masse. Indeed, mass executions characterized every period, with all centuries sharing "a cleansing of occultism" by means of equally wholesale massacres. In 1571 France, under Charles IX, thousands were dispatched on charges and convictions of sorcery. In England, a resulting law passed against witchcraft in 1604, put 70,000 innocents to death.

From Biblical times, onward. Through centuries marked by cultures tied to Babylonia, Greece, Egypt and Rome. Throughout medieval Europe and far into the 18th century, ecclesiastical and royal decrees continuously and categorically, however misplaced, called out: "Thou shalt not practice the evil art of magick."

Uncovered in church and state archives, historical records and personal memoirs, the author offers what he hopes will explain a world rife with fear of the unknown:

Thou shalt not suffer a witch to live.
Exodus 22.18

A man also a woman that hath a familiar spirit, or that is a wizard, shall surely be put to death; they shall stone them with stones; their blood shall be upon them.
Leviticus 20.27

Preface

> But the abominable, and murderers, and Whoremonger, and sorcerers... shall have their part in the lake which burnith with fire and brimstone.
>
> **Revelation 21.8**

> Magicians are those who are commonly called evil-doers on account of the enormity of their crimes. They stir up the elements, disturb men's minds and without any poisonous potion they destroy by the mere force of incantation.
>
> **7th century, Etymologiae**

> ... nor for that reason ought anyone to believe that certain men can perform magic operations without the permission of God.
>
> **Rabanus Maurus, 9th century Abbot of Fulda**

> If either a man or a woman have made magical preparations, and they have been seized in their hands, and charge and proof have been brought against them, the maker of the magical preparation shall be put to death.
>
> **Assyrian Law**

> There is no doubt, as is generally known, that by certain sorceries and demonic illusions they — magicians, soothsayers, seers,

Preface

> sorcerers, diviners, enchanters, interpreters of dreams — so affect the minds of certain people by love philters, food, and prophylactics as to render them mad.
> *Herard, 9th century Archbishop of Tours*

> If a man happens to be a magician, and it is proved against him, he shall be shaven in the form of a cross and scourged and banished.
> *12th century Laws of Forum Turolii, Spain*

> … likewise enchanters, soothsayers, diviners, augurs and magicians, of whatever kind of sex, masters of the magic art and professing that art and those who seek counsel or aid from them, shall be excommunicated.
> *14th century Statutes of Guillaume*

> The art of incantation, divination, augury is abominable to the Lord.
> *15th century Council of Eichstadt*

> Witches must be put to death even though they killed no one by poison; even though they did no harm to crops and beasts; even though they were not necromancers — only because they are leagued with a demon.
> *Martin Delrio, 1599*

Preface

> Sixteen hundred and forty-five, when so many vassals of the Devil were detect'd, that there were thirty try'd at one time, whereas about fourteen were hang'd, and an hundred more detain'd in the prisons of Suffolk and Essex.
>
> **Cotton Mather, 1693**

> Magicians who doom men by curses shalt be destroyed by fire or sword.
>
> **17th century Teutonic Law**

> Those who have made a verbal or written pact and have likewise had abominable intercourse with Satan are wont to be punished by fire.
>
> **17th century [Ecclesiastical] Salute**

> Magicians and witches are to be execrated who by their magic practices not change bodies, by charms and philtres only by sorcery but in strange ways entice men, bewitch by their incantations, drive mad and destroy the unwary, kill brute beasts, contrive disease, hail, noxious air, with the help of a demon, harm cattle and crops, prevent connubial intercourse between man and wife, contrive every kind of harm not by the power of the stars or magic arts, but by a pact and inter-

Preface

course with demons.
17th century Papal Bull

If anyone is convicted of having made a pact with Satan, the enemy of the human race, or of having had any other commerce, even if he has harmed no one… it is deemed that he be burnt alive and driven from our midst in the avenging flames.
18th century Teutonic Law

For over four centuries witch-burnings and hangings, encouraged by ecclesiastical and secular investigations, were prevalent throughout Europe and the American colonies.

The below information was obtained from medieval registries and disheartening witch trial records:

1347-1400
Carcassonne, France: 67 magicians were burned for witchcraft.

1459
Arras, France: A large number of inhabitants — many of whom were simple tricksters — were tortured into confessions of witchcraft. Several were burned.

1482-1486

Preface

> Constance, France: 48 people were convicted of consorting with the Devil and burned.

1507
> Calahorra, Spain: 30 "witches" burned.

1515
> Geneva, Switzerland: Over 500 were executed for witchcraft.

1589
> Saxony, So. East Germany: 133 "witches" were burned in one day.

1591-1600
> Bern, Switzerland: 300 suffered execution for witchcraft.

1627
> Dieburg, Germany: 85 "witches" executed.

1640-1651
> Lindheim, Germany: 30 "witches" burned.

1674-1677
> Mohra, Switzerland: 71 people were beheaded or burned on conviction of witch-

Preface

craft.

1685

The last "witch" executed in England was Alice Molland.

1692

In Salem, Massachusetts, Goody Ann Pudeator [degradingly labeled "Hag of Hell"] was hanged as a "witch," her body tossed into a raging pyre and burned to ashes. Two hundred and sixty-five years later, in 1957, the Massachusetts State Legislature exonerated her of all charges.

1722

The last execution for witchcraft was witnessed in Scotland.

Contents

Preface
Illustrations List
Prologue --- 19

Chapter 1 --- 27
Chapter 2 --- 31
Chapter 3 --- 35
Chapter 4 --- 43
Chapter 5 --- 51
Epilogue --- 55
Illustrations -- 57

Magical Facts & Secrets

Magical Facts
A Case for Showmanship -------------------- 77
A Case for Practice -------------------------- 83

& Secrets
Magician's Secrets --------------------------- 87

Contents

A Magical Glossary

A Magical Glossary ----- 109

Miscellaneous

Chapter Notes ----- 123
Magical Trivia ----- 127
Magical Reading ----- 133

Bibliography ----- 139
Index ----- 143

Illustrations List

Following page 56:

- Jacob Philadelphia (1735-1795).
- Robert-Houdin (1805-1871).
- Robert-Houdin at Chateau St. Cloud, Paris, 1846.
- Alexander Herrmann (1843-1896).
- Title page of Alexander Herrmann's Book of Magic.
- Harry Houdini (1974-1926).
- Rare photograph of Houdini, ca 1915.
- Houdini's favorite portrait of himself.
- Houdini's Death Certificate — filed November 20, 1926.
- Houdini lies in state at the West End Funeral Chapel.
- A mature Bess Houdini (1876-1943).
- Bess and Hardeen [Theo] at Houdini's gravesite, ca 1928.
- Bess Houdini at an early séance. Probably 1927.
- Bess continued attempts to contact her husband…
- Edward Saint, Bess Houdini and Hardeen, 1936.
- Harry Blackstone, Sr. (1885-1965).
- Blackstone baffles Laurel & Hardy, ca 1925-1930.
- **The Great Blackstone** and friends.

Page 131:
- P.T. Selbit performing **Sawing Through A Woman** on a London stage, Jan. 1921.

Prologue

His name was John Ross. The year was 1678.
For John Ross, it would be his final year on earth.
Like many before him, he was to suffer death because a tribunal of inquisitors declared him a male witch. Not a warlock, this should be understood, since that terminology had been outlawed by the courts nearly two centuries before John was born to his merciless world. One was either a male or female witch...

The stout rope, looped around his neck, the extended end pulled by eager arms, chafed as it took him to the place of execution. A cord, wrapped several times around his wrists, gnawed his flesh. Blood oozed from open wounds. Hands from either side grabbed at him, defiled him, as he was hauled forward...

John Ross was the last male witch executed in the Massachusetts Bay in 1678. Though executions of the so-called female witch continued in this colony, as were both sexes throughout Europe, England and diverse New World towns and villages.

Who was John Ross, really? Was he a male witch? Was he "in league with the Devil," as was claimed of him? Or was he one of the innocents caught in a world of conformity to religious opinions?

Perhaps a short look at his life, and the times in which he lived, will give us some answers.

Born in Scotland [1] in 1636, John Ross was forced with his parents and siblings to migrate to the colonies in 1652. They settled in a small community near Salem, Massachusetts.

While John's father plied his trade as a mason to support his growing family, the boy befriended an old man who told him stories of his own youth and taught him the art of manual dexterity. He spoke of times, long passed, when magic was a well-paid profession, when kings and queens commanded amusement by court magicians. Yet religious jealousies would bend the ears of royalty. They were told, "no mere mortals could do the things of these workers of wonders." That only priests, representatives of God, held the sole responsibility for performing miracles. That others who did so represented **The Terrible One — The Prince of Evil — The Father of Lies — The Devil!**

"From those days 'til this," the old man shifted his weight and examined the stump of his left leg, "we have been cursed. Only those magicians close to the church, showing religious

The Magician's Fight!

zeal, were allowed to continue unmolested. The rest were thrown out, maimed or killed! Those who escaped the maimings and killings were forced to perform for table scraps, or to grab what few coins were tossed to them."

The boy looked quizzically at the old man and asked: "If magic is so fearful, why do you do it?

"My father was a conjuror, as was his father before him. I do not work as a conjuror now. Not for years. I live by begging for food and lodging. I'm a coward. While my friends died defending our ancient art, I live because I turned my back on it. I was not strong enough to suffer the pain, nor the death I knew soon would come.

"When I was arrested in 1628, my leg was removed. It was a good leg. There was nothing wrong with it. I was told that my other leg would be taken off unless I revealed the secrets of my magic. If I still refused, I would be put to death as an admitted disciple of Satan. I revealed all! As God is my witness, I told then everything! And showed them that any mortal could do the magic. I'm a coward, boy! I live, but I have died many times inside!"

The boy John Ross, aged 16, begged the old man to teach him all of his magic, vowing never to reveal the secrets — even under the pain of torture, or the menace of death!

And the man John Ross, aged 42, kept his vow…

As flaming torches ignited the dried grass beneath his feet, he suffered in silence. He neither cried out, nor did he plead for mercy.

Slowly, the blaze took and engulfed the body. The crowd backed away. Surely, Satan would claim his own and strike the executioners dead. They turned on their heels and ran. Ran for their lives. Expecting consumption by the very fires now smothering the remains of the "male witch." At the absolute least, they would all be dead by morning.

But, of course, it never happened. They awoke the next morning to a new day.

Nervously, they laughed and cursed their fears of the night before.

As a band, for strength they would have lacked separately, they returned to the place of execution, removed the bones from the still smoldering ashes, and placed them deep into a ground marked for the unholy.

When I commenced researching the historical contents for this work, I spoke with several professional and amateur magicians who enthusiastically allowed me the use of their varied knowledge. One elderly magician distinguished in his own right, Earle Lockman, invited me for a study of two preserved tomes which would help initiate this prologue: **Cases of Conscience Concerning Evil Spirits**, written in 1693 by Increase Mather, and **Innocent Persecutions**, self-published in 1805 by Jeremy Lawrence.

Like two treasures, I carefully examined each book handed me. The workmanship was eminent. The larger of the two volumes — **Cases of Conscience** — was bound with a delicately engraved cover depicting a satanic ritual. Upon cracking it open, my eyes fell immediately to the archaic writing style of the day and I realized a difficult task lay before me.

The second was simpler bound, showing a man or woman

engulfed in flames on a stake, but its interior form provided for easier study.

Having been given permission to take the books home for a time, the next day I seriously set to work.

Cases of Conscience Concerning Evil Spirits traced trials and executions for witchcraft back to the 13th century. Over the years, emphasis was placed on "heretics who, by devilish means, do magick in nonobservance to church teachings." The "heretics" referred to by Reverend Mather were magicians who did not, or would not, conform to unquestionable church doctrine. John Ross was mentioned briefly as "one who shewed [sic] reliance on demons as did no other."

Innocent Persecutions gave an accounting of those who sustained centuries of distress at the hands of illiberal clergymen. From the sinless Joan of Arc and before to the equally blameless John Ross and beyond, the Inquisitions annihilated more human beings than did Attila the Hun's destructive sweep across most of the known world.

Jeremy Lawrence wrote he was a direct descendant of John Ross, defending his forebear's ability as a clever conjuror. "Satan," he argued, "did not give my ancestor power. Only by diligence and practise [sic] did he perfect his miracles."

Ironically, within two days of John Ross's execution, the royal governor of Massachusetts Bay, John Leverett, issued a decree exempting male witches from prosecution in his colony.

Unfortunately, his successor, Simon Bradstreet, dismissed the order in 1679 and the killings continued for both sexes in this province and all colonies throughout America. Raking further across every part of the world.

The conjuror was forced to seek refuge. To hide as a hermit. Awaiting victory over this oppression [2]...

The Magician's Fight!

"…but as records of courts and justice are admissible, it can easily be proved that powerful and malevolent magicians once existed and were a scourge to mankind…"
Ambrose Bierce
The Devil's Dictionary
(1842 – ca 1914)

Chapter 1

In 2570 B.C.E., a man stood before the court of a king and performed miracles baffling the most learned men present.

From a goose he removed the head, then restored it. Other decapitations and restorations followed until an ox was dismembered and, with a mighty incantation shaking even the heavens, was again made whole.

This man was 110-year-old Dedi of Ded-Snefru. The king was Kheops, 2nd pharaoh, 4th Dynasty Egypt [1].

Magic had its beginnings thousands of years prior to his time, yet with Dedi came the true-recorded history of the art of magic. Foregoing him, troubadours sang of the "miracles of the magi," embellishing to such an extent it is hard to separate fact from fiction. Dedi, however, actually administered his miracles through sleight of hand [2] and misdirection.

Centuries passed. Times changed. Magic darkened synonymous with witchcraft. Sleight of hand performers, once hailed by kings and immortalized through song and verse, were now cursed as the Devil's own. In 1226 C.E., a proclamation, cast by Louis IX of France, asserted "No magician ....shalt enter my kingdom," fearing they would encourage "evil habits among the people." Other countries soon followed. The magician was outlawed. The rich, flowing robes of the court magician gave way to the dust-ridden rags of the conjuror or "mountebank" — a derisively coined phrase for charlatan.

These conjurors would do anything from the classically old **cups and balls** to sword swallowing and fire-breathing. They would mount a platform or dirt bank and perform their wonders, passing a grubby hat for any bit of change offered after each completion.

Unhappily, though, they were often chased away or arrested by local gendarmes before concluding their show. In 1571, a conjuror that staged simple card tricks was seized in Paris on charges of male witchery, convicted of employing "demonic assistance" and executed. The dark ages for magic had begun!

Executions pursued the outlawed "wonder worker" into the 18th century. Witch-hunts of Europe, Great Britain and America eliminated more inoffensive magical entertainers than did they the so-called witch. Many conjurors, to save themselves, revealed their secrets, thus ending their livelihood. Those who refused — died!

But the conjuror was not a witch. He was a skilled performer. A master in the art of harmless deception.

The Magician's Fight!

He began to fight for his art!

On April 14, 1735 in Philadelphia, Pennsylvania, was born someone who was to lead that fight. Jacob Meyer, upon his conversion to Christianity, took the unlikely name of **Philadelphia** in homage to leading businessman and scientist— Benjamin Franklin of his hometown— and toured Europe presenting his "scientific" magic, giving command performances before such dignitaries as Catherine II of Russia, Frederick the Great in Potsdam [3] and Sultan Mustapha III in Constantinople.

His knowledge of physics and mathematics secured him an edge over any competition, and his expert showmanship built his reputation. His **séances** consisted of mysticism and pseudo-scientific mumbo-jumbo. His tricks were called **experiments**, while his sleights were hidden beneath a cloak of **scientific equipment**.

Those who studied physics called him professor. Those who thought him a male witch feared his wrath should they dare make that accusation. Such was his believed power. He could not be touched.

After amassing a fortune, he retired stately to private life.

In 1774, he wrote a pamphlet entitled ***Little Treatise on Strange and Appropriate Feats***, believed the earliest known published work on magic authored by an American.

Philadelphia had paved the way. Dr. Gustavus Katterfelto, a quack doctor and conjuror of this same period, had tried with **scientific experiments** of his own, but lacked the showmanship and compelling air displayed by Philadelphia, thus failing to bring about the changes of his colleague.

Not long before his death in the small market town of Bedale, North Yorkshire County, England on November 25, 1799, he was jailed as a "vagabond and imposter."

Others followed in the wake of Jacob Philadelphia…

Renewed appearances, from welcomed social gatherings to courts of royalty, energized the conjuror's confidence. He came from concealment to take his place amidst a society having ousted and persecuted him for so many centuries.
He would never again hide from that society!

Chapter 2

Jean Eugene Robert grew to manhood marveling at the wonders of this new breed of conjuror. Though a clockmaker by trade, he enjoyed magic as a hobby. Count Edmund de Grisy, known as Torrini, last of the itinerant conjurors, would shift that hobby into high gear in 1828.

Robert had been stricken with food poisoning, having eaten a hearty meal of tainted beef stew, and was wandering delirously along the roadside when he was picked up by Torrini, nursed back to health, and taught the latest methods in magical sleights and gestures.

Torrini himself, clicking his horse and traveling wagon, had been ambling along in his own delirium when he spotted the young man. In 1826 he had accidentally shot his son, Giovanni, exhibiting the dangerous **Bullet Catch** trick he claimed and named **Son of William Tell**, in which a marked bullet would find its way into an apple held in his son's mouth. Nearly two years had passed and he still could not shake the madness tearing at his mind. He spent six months in jail. His wife had died of grief. His career had fallen to crumbs.

But these mattered little. He had killed his own son!

Tears streamed his face as he raised the young man to a sitting position and coaxed him into drinking a stomach-discharging concoction. In his raving, fevered thoughts he saw his only son. He could not lose him again!

Unknowingly, this gentle old magician, in an attempt to release a consumptive guilt, had awarded the world of magic another leader. A man who would someday be recognized as "the father of modern magic" — Robert-Houdin [pronounced Robear-Hoodin]. [1]

Robert, however, was not known by that name until he married Joséphe Cécile Houdin in 1830, hyphenating his surname to her's.

Robert-Houdin was not only a skilled performer. He was an ingenious innovator. Though many of the enchanting inventions asserted in his autobiography were not his, a controversy raised by Harry Houdini in **The Unmasking of Robert-Houdin,** we must recognize his novel approach to the inventions of others as having added immeasurably to the art.

On July 3, 1845, Robert-Houdin opened his theater of magic, **Soirées Fantastique** at the Palais Royal in Paris, fulfilling a lifelong dream. During this time, he was at his best. With his young son Emile [and later his younger son Eugene] by his side, he performed to the delight and ovation of audiences who had shunned the very word "magic" but a short time earlier.

Unfortunately, the second revolution of 1848 closed Pal-

The Magician's Fight!

ais Royal, yet **Soirées Fantastique** had initiated a paragon which would remain to this day for those who wished it. The magician was taken from the streets and settled in a theater either hired or owned by himself.

Closing the theaters in France did not dampen Robert-Houdin's determined spirit, however. He went to England. From there he successfully toured Ireland, Scotland, Belgium and Germany, waiting for his homeland to resume a somewhat normal status.

Upon returning home, he reopened **Soirées Fantastique** at Palais Royal and continued there until his formal retirement in 1851.

Pierre Chocat, adopting the stage name Hamilton, later took over the hall and captivated Parisian audiences with his brother-in-law's identical mysteries. [2]

Robert-Houdin spent his retirement years conducting mechanical and electrical experiments. In 1851, he publicly demonstrated incandescent light bulbs at his estate in Blois, France. [3]

In 1856, he was sent on a special mission by Emperor Napoleon III to Algeria, French North Africa, where he quelled a potential uprising induced by a cult of Islamic sorcerers known as the Marabouts. In proving French magic's superior strength, he was ceremoniously decorated by his government.

His last years were spent in study and the writing of books, of which *Les Secrets de La Prestidigitation et de La*

James Charles Bouffard, Psy.D., Ph.D.

Magie [translated by magician-author Professor Louis Hoffman to read: ***The Secrets of Conjuring and Magic***] was considered his best.

Robert-Houdin died of pneumonia on June 13, 1871 at St. Gervais, a suburb of his birthplace Blois, at the age of 65. He had lived a full and useful life.

In 1881, Blois paid homage by renaming one of its little streets: **Rue Robert-Houdin**.

In 1971, France issued a postage stamp honoring her nation's greatest magician.

Chapter 3

Though many claimed succession to Robert-Houdin only one stood separate from the rest, and in so doing succeeded him in fame.

Alexander Herrmann was 28 when Robert-Houdin died and was already moving toward the title of Herrmann the Great. A title not self-allotted, rather bestowed upon him by Czar Alexander III during a Russian engagement and banquet in 1884.

Alexander Herrmann was born in Paris, France on February 11, 1843 of German-Jewish heritage on his paternal side. His mother was a pure Breton Frenchwoman. Their union produced sixteen children — of whom eight were boys. Alexander was the youngest. His brother, Carl, the oldest.

Carl [Compars] Herrmann was born in Hanover, Germany on January 25, 1816. He, too, was an accomplished magician, rivaling Robert-Houdin during the latter's lifetime. In 1853, he stole Alexander away from home and brought him to St. Petersburg, Russia to serve as his apprentice during a command performance. While there, he tutored the boy on the many feats of legerdemain, which would later deliver him to renown.

Their father, Samuel, bitterly opposed. He was a physician who practiced prestidigitation for his own amusement, wishing none of his children to follow it professionally. He had wanted Carl to pursue a medical career. Now he was to lose any thought of Alexander amounting to more than a vagabond. Their mother was sent to bring the boy home to Paris. She succeeded, but could only postpone the inevitable.

In 1855, Alexander was off again in search of his brother. They met in Vienna and remained together until Alexander decided to try it alone. He went to Spain and was invited to debut before Her Majesty, Queen Isabella II. It was 1858. He was fifteen years of age. From there, he toured the world.

In 1860, Alexander entered America as Carl's assistant. Their booking at the Academy of Music [Star Theater], in Brooklyn, NY sold every seat for seventy-five nights.

In a subsequent agreement, the brothers divided the hemisphere between them.

Carl rarely returned to the United States, though Alexander continued traveling Europe. As well as both North and South America.

The Magician's Fight!

Alexander Herrmann was an imposing figure. Tall and slender, his appearance reminded one of Mephistopheles in the Faust tradition. His distinctive imperial beard with swooping mustache, his long straight nose topped with penatrating black eyes, gave observers to fear an inferno would erupt at any moment. But it never did. Herrmann would display a broad, pleasant smile and hold out a skilled hand to anyone who would approach. His gentleness and kindly airs were well known.

Still, notwithstanding his true character offstage, onstage Herrmann enacted the prince of evil with every gesture and movement. He gave his audience the fantastically unreal. The supernatural powers of the world below! This he did with a sly wink and an impish tilt of his head as wonder after wonder unfolded before the eyes of his gaping onlookers. He was no mere mortal, this great Alexander Herrmann, who appeared on stage in a blaze of fire and vanished from it in that same diabolical splendor. Satan was here on Earth, and her people loved him.

Herrmann's satanic demeanor once prompted a friend, actor Louis Morrison, to play a practical joke on him. It was during a performance at the Tabor Opera House, Denver, Colorado in 1894. Herrmann had just completed one of his most baffling illusions and gracefully bowed, awaiting applause. Nothing! His audience, instead, was looking away. Toward the back-center of the stage. Herrmann followed their gaze, almost losing his footing in doing so. For there, centered on the stage, stood the cloaked figure of evil. His arms folded across his chest, as if expecting an explanation for this affront to his worldly rule. He then began to laugh. A low, sinister laugh at first, rising to a high, jovial chortling. "I hope I did not give you too much of a fright, my friend," chuckled Morrison. "I guess now you know how we feel."

The audience roared. Herrmann sniggered, but it was clear he was shaken. The curtains were immediately rung down and he went to his dressing room. Next day, he and his company left Denver.

Morrison would always feel this joke helped effectuate Herrmann's fatal heart attack two years later. Whether or not this was so, the fact remains he never played a practical joke on anyone after the magician's death.

Herrmann, nevertheless, was not opposed to good, harmless jokes. He would often produce a live chicken from the hat of a man he had just met on the street. And a lady would delight when he handed her a live rose plucked from the center of her imitation-flowered bonnet. Once, upon an introduction to Ulysses S. Grant, he reached over and pulled a handful of the president's favorite cigars from his shaggy whiskers. Thus, securing a life-long friendship. In such a manner, for all virtual purposes, these were the nature of Alexander Herrmann's practical jokes.

In 1875, Herrmann married Adelaide Scarcez, a beautiful 22-year-old ballerina who added charm and grace to the mysterious surroundings on stage. She would grow to function as his indispensable assistant and partner. In 1887, he told a reporter in an interview: "Wherever I go, Madame Herrmann goes. We have been married twelve years now, and we are never apart. I do not believe that I could work without her

The Magician's Fight!

now; I am so used to her help." More than "used to her help," he hinged upon her. He was beside himself with worry if his "little Adie" had the slightest cold, and he could not function greater than a passable showing if she was not on stage with him. "She is a gem," he closed the interview.

Herrmann gave his all to the art of magic. Many of his exhibitions were for charity, or for the amusement of young children confined to hospital beds. He would persistently rush from the completion of a paid engagement to a charity affair given that same night. This eventually wore on his already weak heart to the extent he would gasp for breath and grab for his chest whenever overly excited. Adelaide Herrmann's self-appointed job was to keep him as calm as possible. A considerably difficult task.

On Wednesday, December 16, 1896, the 53-year-old magician appeared at the Lyceum Theater, Rochester, NY. Next day, he clutched his chest for the last time in his private railroad car en route from Rochester to Bradford, PA. Adelaide was by his side. His final words to her were: "I guess I'm not going to get over this. Take the company back to New York." The news spread. And that day — December 17, 1896 — the world knew Herrmann the Great was dead.

On Sunday, December 20th, he was laid to rest in Woodlawn Cemetery, New York City, as friends and admirers, numbering thousands, bowed their heads in quiet respect.

The following pages contain a New York Times article of December 18, 1896:

James Charles Bouffard, Psy.D., Ph.D.

The New York Times
Published: December 18, 1896
Copyright © The New York Times

MAGICIAN HERRMANN DEAD

HE BREATHES HIS LAST IN HIS PRIVATE RAILROAD CAR.

Apparently in Good Health When He Left Rochester Yesterday Morning — The End Came Suddenly.

Rochester, N.Y., Dec. 17. — Alexander Herrmann, the magician, who appeared at the Lyceum Theatre last night, concluding an engagement of three performances, died this morning in his private car while on the Buffalo, Rochester, and Pittsburgh Road on his way to Bradford, Penn., where he was to open an engagement this evening.

Prof. Herrmann was well as usual when he left this city this morning at 7: 30 o'clock. He had passed the night in his private car, and was in bed when word was sent from it to the station master at Great Valley that he was ill, and the attendance of a physician was desired. Before a physician could

The Magician's Fight!

get to the car Herrmann was dead. The car was taken on to Salamanca with the body. It is not yet known in this city what caused the magician's death. When he took leave of Manager Pierce of the Lyceum after the performance last night, he was in apparently perfect health. He was entertained at the Genesee Valley Club later, and seemed to be all right when accompanied to his special car by several of his Rochester friends.

One of the last acts of Mr. Herrmann was to extend financial aid to a stranded theatrical company in this city. The "American Cousin Company" broke up at the Academy here last week, and yesterday Mr. Herrmann was made aware of the fact and immediately telephoned the hotel where the company were stopping to send him the bill of $50, and to tell all the members to come to his show last night and he would have their railroad tickets to New York [City] all ready for them.

Last night after the performance some one asked Mr. Herrmann who would be his successor in case anything should happen to him. He said he had a nephew [Leon Herrmann] in Paris he was very anxious to have learn the art, and he said that he intended to go to Paris next Summer to see him. This nephew, he said, is studying law, and he did not want him to give it up.

His Chief Attraction: Frankness

Herrmann's chief attraction to many people was his frank denial that magic [witchery] or supernatural powers had anything to do with his exhibitions. It was he who gave a dignified meaning to the cant word prestidigitateur, by which he preferred to be called. He was a man of sympathetic temperment, and spent large sums annually in aid of unfortunate theatrical people. On the day before his death, he gave a benefit performance for the waifs of the State Industrial School at Rochester.

He was to have opened a week's engagement in the Great Northern Theater, Chicago, Monday night. The private car bearing his body will reach New York on the Erie Road at 6:40 o'clock this morning.

Chapter 4

With Alexander Herrmann and after came other exceptional magicians: Adelaide Herrmann [Alexander's widow], Leon Herrmann [Alexander's nephew], Harry Keller, Chung Ling Soo [William Ellsworth Robinson], Harry Houdini…

Houdini

On Sunday morning, October 31, 1926, in Room 401, Grace Hospital, Detroit, Michigan, Harry Houdini whispered to his brother: "Dash… I'm tired of fighting. I guess this thing is going to get me." Beatrice Houdini, weakened with shock, was wheeled to his bedside. She leaned over and clung to him, as if trying to keep the man she had loved for thirty-two years from leaving. But it was of no use. Subsequent to 7 days, and two operations, the septicemia created by advanced peritonitis sapped strength from his body. At 1:26 p.m., on the afternoon of the celebration of Halloween, he closed his eyes in eternal sleep.

James Charles Bouffard, Psy.D., Ph.D.

Houdini was born Ehrich Weiss in Budapest, Hungary on March 24, 1874 [1].

Following his birth, the family fled to America and settled in Appleton, Wisconsin until 1883; the year Ehrich's father, Mayer Samuel, lost his post as Appleton's first rabbi, at a salary of $750 per year, and the household was forced to uproot to Milwaukee.

Times were wearisome for the Weisses. Between 1883 and 1885, they had packed up and moved from one Milwaukee address to another on at least five occasions — racing to keep one step ahead of the rent collector. "Such hardships became our lot," Houdini would later write.

In 1886, Ehrich left home in an attempt to help the house income, but found employment difficult for a 12-year-old boy. Meanwhile, Samuel took heart and left for New York City in his own endeavor to eliminate the crises. As in a storybook romance, he and Ehrich found each other in a boardinghouse on East 79th Street, and together they earned and saved enough money to bring the entire family from Wisconsin. The year was 1888. Samuel and Ehrich introduced them to their new address on East 75th Street.

They lived there — "I mean starved there," wrote Houdini, "for several years." From there, they moved to 305 East 69th Street. This was their final stop. They would remain at this address without another inconvenient move.

The Magician's Fight!

Although Ehrich was keenly interested in magic from early boyhood, it wasn't until he rescued a copy of Robert-Houdin's autobiography from a second-hand bookstore that this interest evolved into an obsession. For days, weeks, he read and dreamed. He would be a magician. And why not? Wasn't his heritage in the country of mystery, legend and magic? Didn't vampires, werewolves and "things that go bump in the night" roam the land of his ancestors? It was his birthright. He would be a magician!

With practice in the art of sleight of hand under the tutorage of Jacob Hyman, [2] a fellow employee at H. Richter's Sons Necktie Factory and an amateur magician, young Ehrich styled himself "Eric the Great." Every now and then he would stage a little show for his public. And sometimes, more then than now, would receive payment for it. "As youse can see, I ain't got nut' in up my sleeve," the gleeful little wizard would open his act.

In 1891, Ehrich would change his name altogether. Hyman, by now Eric the Great's frequent assistant, suggested an "i" on the end of a surname meant "like." And, as Ehrich's idol was still Robert-Houdin — and he wished to be "like him" — he added an "i" to Houdin.

His parents called him Ehrich. To everyone else he was "Ehrie," — which sounded like "Harry" — so, to simplify matters, he spelled the name: H-a-r-r-y. The perfect prelude to his new moniker.

Later, Harry and Jacob named themselves the "Houdini

Brothers." Still later, Jacob left the team and was replaced by Harry's real brother, Theo.

No longer plain Eric the Great, 17-year-old Harry Houdini decided he was ready for the "big time" and quit his job at H. Richter's Sons.

Egotistical and ill tempered by some accounts, kind and generous by other reports, Houdini was both. And he made it to the top as both. Not, however, as a professional magician. His visions of replicating Robert-Houdin faded soon after bidding his family farewell with a promise to someday spread his fortune at the feet of his tearful, adored mother.

Unfortunately, three years of drifting from one sideshow to another, from one poor engagement to one even shabbier, brought one old suit, crackers and milk for dinner — and a wife. Not a very good start. He had a long way to go if he was to make good his promise.

What he needed was an act entirely different. Something to make him immortal. Something to show the "wisenheimers" who had laughed when he called himself "The King of Cards."

Having apprenticed as a locksmith for a short period at the tender age of eleven, he opted to use and improve on his learning. He would be, now and for all time, "Houdini, The Handcuff King, the greatest escape artist the world will ever know." It satisfied his ego to think himself elevated to such a magnitude. Now he had to prove it!

His young wife, Bess, went along with anything her excit-

The Magician's Fight!

able husband came up with, provided she stood in the limelight with him. When he got there!

Houdini met Wilhelmina Beatrice Rahner in 1894 through his brother, Dash [3], when the young men worked Coney Island as "The Brothers Houdini." They fell hopelessly in love and, following a brief courtship, were married on June 22, 1894 in a civil ceremony. She was 18. He was 20. As Bess was Catholic and Harry Jewish, they were subsequently wedded by a priest and rabbi. "I'm the most married woman I know," she would joke. "Three times! To the same man!"

Houdini's initial presentations as an escape artist were combined with magic. Card tricks, silk effects, and his even then well-known **Metamorphosis** were closed with a challenge to escape any pair of handcuffs proffered by a member or members of his audience. A small, but effective, beginning.
Effective, yes. For the small circuits. The big shows wouldn't have him. Martin Beck, booker for the Orpheum Vaudeville chain and "Mr. Show Business of the West," was to change that. "You're overdoing your act," he wrote to him by telegraph. "When you do escapes. Do escapes! Don't clutter your act with other, nonessential hocus-pocus. It confuses an audience. On the other hand, when you do magic, concentrate on magic. If you wish to work for me, I'll insist that your act consist of two effects. The trunk escape [**Metamorphosis**] and the handcuff challenge."
Houdini quickly agreed, and the team of Harry and Bess

Houdini made its official debut in the spring of 1899. At $60 per week.

From that year unadulterated triumph followed. Houdini did spread his fortune [figuratively — in gold coins] at his mother's feet. He did show the "wisenheimers" that had laughed when he called himself "The King of Cards." And he did become the greatest escape artist the world will ever know.

We leave it for generations to determine whether his inopportune death from a ruptured appendix at the age of 52 was meant to accord him the immortality he so craved, or whether Death was angered by a magician who had cheated him for so long a time.

He was placed in the bronze coffin used to outdo Egyptian magician Rahman Bey's "living burial." Below his head was laid a black bag containing his mother's letters. Above his grave in the Machpelah Cemetery, Ridgewood, Queens County, New York, stands a monument to his greatness — designed by himself [4].

As the casket was lowered slowly into the earth one of his pallbearers, showman Florenz Ziegfeld, was heard to utter: "Suppose he isn't in it!"

Bess Houdini would hold annual séances in attempts to contact her husband's spirit. On October 31, 1936, following a last unsuccessful séance conducted on the roof of the old Knickerbocker Hotel, Hollywood, California, she sadly extinguished a candle kept burning throughout each sitting.

The Magician's Fight!

"Houdini did not come through to me," she solemnly said as she put out the flame. "My last hope is gone. I do not believe that Houdini can come back to me. Or to anyone. It is finished. Good night, Harry!"

Shortly before succumbing to cancer and a lung ailment on February 11, 1943, though, she found humor for a quip to the media: "Ten years is long enough to wait for any man."

The séances were eventually reanimated and continue to this day by magicians all over the world on each Halloween.

Still in hopes for a visit from Houdini.

James Charles Bouffard, Psy.D., Ph.D.

"How the priests came into possession of these secrets does not appear, and if there were ever any records of this kind the Church would hardly allow them to become public."
Harry Houdini
(1874 – 1926)

Chapter 5

Stunned and saddened by **The Master's** death was one Harry Bouton, better known as **The Great Blackstone**. To him, as with many, Houdini was invincible. Death did not know him; therefore, could never lay claim!

Blackstone was born Henri Boughton in Chicago, Illinois on September 27, 1885. Henri was changed to Harry [1] and Boughton shortened to Bouton when he and his brother, Pete, styled themselves "The Bouton Brothers, Straight and Crooked Magic." Harry would affect straight magic, while Pete added comedy to the act by trying to "outmagic" his brother.

Harry had always dreamed of starting in big. Small exhibitions would not be enough. Gala extravaganzas were in his visions. His shows would wax large. Marvelously large! Pete was unable to comprehend any of this, so the two splintered what could have been a profitable and immortal union.

Pete remained relatively unknown, while Harry went on to

James Charles Bouffard, Psy.D., Ph.D.

rise as **The Dean of American Stage Illusionists**.

Harry's first solo stage character was that of Frederick the Great. This happened, according to George Boston [2], when the young man visited a printer to order posters for one of his shows and found an unclaimed bundle of papers marked for a magician named Frederick. Eagerly, he scooped up the bills and changed his name. Later, upon commencing his full-evening shows, he would rename himself once more. This time to Harry Blackstone.

During the 1930s and '40s, Blackstone reigned supreme over all other magicians in America. With his bushy dark hair now grown an impressive white, he dazzled his audiences with a quick rush onto the stage, his black cape sailing behind him, and issuing forth a panorama of spitfire productions.

The pace would lessen, then cease. Walking toward the front of the stage, speaking for the first time, he would ask for a man's handkerchief — preferably an unused one. A stretch of the cloth and a knot was tied in one end to represent the head. Suddenly, it would jump from the magician's hands and dance around the stage. Blackstone giving chase. Ah, captured! The handkerchief — now a spook — again in the hands of the magician, wriggled and twisted to get away. The owner was requested to take back his handkerchief, whereupon it lost its magical vitality and was once more an ordinary piece of cloth.

This was one of Blackstone's most noted feats, though he

The Magician's Fight!

produced and vanished beautiful young ladies with remarkable adeptness.

Any accomplished magician could do the **Dancing Handkerchief** [3], however it took Blackstone's excellent showmanship to guide it through to its beguiling conclusion.

In September of 1942, Blackstone performed what many believe his greatest magical accomplishment: **The Vanishing Audience**.

During a performance at the Lincoln Theater, Decatur, Illinois, he learned that a fire had broken out in the Rambo Drugstore adjoining the theater, endangering the auditorium with smoke and a possible blaze. Calmly, he announced that his next trick was so large, so spectacular; all members of his audience would have to adjourn to the street to properly view it. Blackstone then smilingly organized an orderly, row-by-row exit through the alley doors and down the balcony steps. Once on the street, each turned to witness the surrounding buildings engulfed in flames. Little damage was done to the newly fireproofed theater itself, but in his coolness Blackstone had saved nearly one thousand schoolchildren, plus numerous adults, by averting a deadly panic.

Radio listeners of the late '40s and early '50s heard the voice of Blackstone. Television viewers of the late '50s and early '60s saw the face of Blackstone. And comic book fans of that era thrilled to his fictional adventures.

Blackstone's series of radio shows captivated listeners in that limbo between reality and the realm of the unknown.

And he was the only real-life magician designated a superhero.

Harry Blackstone, looking back on his accomplishments and smiling at the heights to which he had helped to lift the art of magic [4], retired to his home in Hollywood, California, where he passed peacefully away on November 16, 1965 at the age of 80.

His ashes were conveyed to his former hometown of Colon, Michigan [5] and interred in Lakeside Cemetery, famous as **The Final Act** for many well-known magical entertainers.

As greatness goes, there was no one equal to Harry Blackstone, yet there was one destined to succeed him.

His name was Harry Blackstone, Jr., magician, author and star of the longest-running magical extravaganza on Broadway to date. Although he submitted to complications of pancreatic cancer at the early age of sixty-two on May 14, 1997, the gifted son and heir to **The Great Blackstone** will forever remain in our minds and hearts.

Out of the darkness into the light came the magician. The long struggle had culminated in victory. The magicians of today owe their absolute existence to our striving wonder-workers of yesterday. For without them, there would have been no magic. And a world without magic would be like a world without children — of all ages!

Epilogue

What placed Jacob Philadelphia, Robert-Houdin, Alexander Herrmann, Harry Houdini and Harry Blackstone, Sr. a cut above other exceptional magicians of their time? And what afforded them the leadership qualities to pull the art of magic from the black hole determined to bury it?

In order to answer these questions, we must first look toward the one ingredient essential to the make-up of all performers and performances. **Showmanship!**

To quote Harry Houdini: "Showmanship, for all intents and purposes, is doing something on a larger scale than the average person would do it."

So we observe these leaders to have carried the art of magic to its victory through a perceptive need to become greater showmen. While other, perhaps better, magicians relied less upon showmanship and looked more toward their perfected skills. Sadly, many of these talented conjurors are known solely to students of the art and forgotten by the general public.

James Charles Bouffard, Psy.D., Ph.D.

According to research, Dr. Katterfelto far exceeded Jacob Philadelphia in manipulative skills. Yet he continued to wear the rags of a street conjuror, while Philadelphia gave back the elegant attire of the court magician. What about Robert-Houdin? Did he have any rivals? He had many. Who remembers them? And who speaks of Carl when the name Herrmann is mentioned? Doesn't Alexander come to mind? By numerous accounts, Carl far surpassed his brother in deftness. And who, but someone in the magic circle, has ever referred to Horace Goldin in conversation? Yet, he was doing well during Houdini's time. And Harry Blackstone, Sr.? **The Dean of American Stage Illusionists** will outlive us all — years into the future!

Interestingly, when news of **The Great Blackstone**'s passing reached the editorial offices of **The New Tops** conjuror's magazine, they wrote this short but unforgettable tribute:

"Harry Blackstone, age 80.
Occupation: Legend."

**Jacob Philadelphia
(1735 – 1795)**
(Image in author's collection)

Robert-Houdin
(1805 – 1871)
(Image in author's collection)

Robert-Houdin at Chateau St. Cloud, Paris, 1846.
(Image courtesy: Library of Congress)

**Alexander Herrmann
(1843 – 1896)**
(Image in author's collection)

Herrmann's Book of Magic
Black Art Fully Exposed

A COMPLETE AND PRACTICAL GUIDE TO DRAWING-ROOM AND STAGE MAGIC FOR PROFESSIONALS AND AMATEURS, INCLUDING A COMPLETE EXPOSURE OF THE BLACK ART.

BY
PROF. HERRMANN.

FULLY ILLUSTRATED.

Chicago
FREDERICK J. DRAKE & COMPANY
Publishers

**Title page to Alexander Herrmann's Book of Magic.
[Published posthumously in 1903.]**
(Image in author's collection)

**Harry Houdini
(1874 – 1926)**
(Image in author's collection)

Rare photograph of Houdini, ca 1915.
(Courtesy: Geoffrey Hansen collection)

Houdini's favorite portrait of himself.
(Image courtesy: Smithsonian Institute)

Houdini's Death Certificate—filed November 20, 1926.
Proponents to the belief Houdini died of poisoning by galled spiritualists who wished revenge on the magician, and not of a ruptured appendix, base their arguments on "discrepancies" in this certificate. Discrepancies, which this author has not found. (Image courtesy: Library of Congress)

MASTER WIZARD STILL IN DEATH—Harry Houdini, who for years held first rank among stage magicians, and earned wide and well-merited fame as a ruthless foe and exposer of charlatans and spiritualistic "mediums", died at Detroit, Michigan, while on tour a short time ago. His remains were prepared for burial by W. R. Hamilton & Company, of Detroit, and forwarded to New York City, where they were received by Samuel Rothschild. For two days they lay in state in Mr. Rothschild's establishment, the West End Funeral Chapel, while notables from the theatrical world visited the mortuary to pay their respects. Flowers in great profusion were sent by members of the profession and the dead magician's host of personal friends, three full cars being required to convey the floral tributes to the cemetery. The casket used for interment was a Boyertown solid bronze, and an hermetically sealed inner liner, made especially for Mr. Houdini, for use in his stage performances by the Boyertown Burial Casket Company last summer, was used to enclose the body inside the outer case of bronze. It is estimated that considerably more than a thousand people passed by the remains as they lay in state in Mr. Rothschild's mortuary.

Houdini lies in state at the West End Funeral Chapel, New York City. (Image courtesy: Fred Sneathern)

**A mature Bess Houdini
(1876 – 1943)
Still pained by the death of her husband.**
(Image courtesy: Houdini Museum)

Bess and Hardeen [Theo] at Houdini's gravesite, ca 1928.
(Image courtesy: Robert R. King/houdinitribute.com)

Bess Houdini at an early séance. Probably 1927.
(Image in author's collection)

Bess Houdini continued attempts to contact her husband on Halloween for 10 years of his death. (Image courtesy: Library of Congress.)

Edward Saint [left], Bess Houdini and Hardeen, 1936.
This photograph was taken several moments prior to Bess' last attempt to reach her husband, conducted on the roof of the Knickerbocker Hotel, Hollywood, California. Dr. Saint, a former vaudeville showman and magician, assisted her in this final "spirit test." (Image courtesy: Library of Congress)

**Harry Blackstone, Sr.
(1885 – 1965)**
(Image in author's collection)

Blackstone baffles Laurel & Hardy, ca 1925 – 1930.
(Image courtesy: Laurel & Hardy Central Museum)
From a donation by: M.J. Enigh
[Magician and Entertainer]

The Great Blackstone and friends.
(Image in author's collection)

Magical Facts
&
Secrets

"Yet to-day, if a mystifier lacks the ingenuity to invent a new and startling stunt, he can safely fall back upon a trick that has been a favorite of press agents the world over in all ages — **showmanship!**"
Harry Houdini
(1874 – 1926)

Magical Facts

A Case for Showmanship

In 1765, prior to moving to Germany for an extensive and prosperous European tour, Jacob Philadelphia was reported to have entered the city of his birth simultaneously from north and south. This piece of showmanship secured for him the reputation of a true wizard.

One hundred and forty-two years later Harry Houdini unknowingly did Philadelphia one better:

The date: June 10, 1907. The place: New York City. Houdini plays before a vast audience at New York's **Hippodrome Theater**...

The date: June 10, 1907. The place: Philadelphia, Pennsylvania. Houdini is seen at the **Walnut Street Theater**...

Impossible! No one could be in two places, one hundred miles apart, on the same day in those slow-moving times. Or could they?

James Charles Bouffard, Psy.D., Ph.D.

Harry Houdini could and was in the form, in Philadelphia, of brother Dash [Theo], his only legal imitator.

Dash, known as Hardeen, bore a striking resemblance to his brother at that time and was often mistaken for him. As Houdini was billed to feature in both New York City and Philadelphia on June 10th, the budding master showman devised a scheme to keep the two theaters happy while adding to his reputation. Dash would take the role of "Harry Houdini" in Philadelphia, while he — the genuine article — appeared in the illustrious city of New York. Each would enter their respective locale at precisely the same time, with identical acts. The papers in both New York City and Philadelphia reported seeing "The remarkable Harry Houdini" — dated June 10, 1907.

A swindle? Not at all! A classic piece of showmanship!

"The secret of showmanship," wrote Houdini in his **Unmasking of Robert-Houdin**, "consists not of what you really do, but of what the mystery-loving public thinks you do."

When Houdini resumed performing stage magic, he revised an accomplished little effect from his vaudeville days.

The East Indian Needle Mystery:

Houdini would swallow several dozen large sewing needles, along with a giant wad of white thread and a mouthful of water. Shortly, the end of the thread would appear between his lips and stretched across the stage, the needles glimmering at interval along the thread.

As a magical effect, **The Needle Trick** [as it is now call-

The Magician's Fight!

ed] in itself is silly. When done by the average performer, it really doesn't make much sense. Do the needles thread themselves in the magician's mouth, or stomach? Does the magician thread the needles with his tongue? This would be more tongue juggling than a deed of magic. Houdini, however, turned this meaningless bit of legerdemain into an important and impressive stage illusion through his superb showmanship.

Let us take a look at just how he did it:

Houdini invites twenty spectators from the audience to assist him in his latest "magical endeavor." A dentist is also escorted onto the stage by Bess, and requested to examine the magician's mouth. A dental mirror is provided for this.

Following the examination, the twenty "assistants" are positioned behind Houdini as he places one, then two packets of large sewing needles into his mouth and swallows. Approximately thirty-five feet of white thread is then wadded, placed in his mouth, and washed down with a glass of water.

With the sound of soft music rising to a crescendo from the orchestra, an end of the thread looms betwixt Houdini's lips. Bess has one of the "assistants" take hold of this end and pull. A bell resounds as a needle emerges, gleaming, on the thread. The thread is pulled out further. A bell tinkles. Further and further, the thread is pulled out, a needle shining with each ting of a bell. Clear across the stage, the thread is stretched slowly. Five, ten, twelve minutes pass. The audience is held spellbound. A drum roll is heard, and the last of the thread is drawn from Houdini's mouth and raised aloft by the magician and his "assistant." Houdini walks toward the footlights and bows to thunderous applause.

Without a need to divulge the trick's actual method, let us now study what Houdini did that was different:

First— The twenty "assistants" were used simply to fashion a large production from a diminutive effect. There was no other reason for their presence on the stage.

Second— Having a dentist examine his mouth was just something fancied by Houdini to lend authenticity.

Third— He used two packets of needles. The average performer uses one. [Depending on the size of his audience, he used as many as one hundred needles.]

Fourth— The average performer uses six feet of thread at the most. Houdini was satisfied with no less than thirty-five feet. [Again, depending on audience size, the length of thread increased. At the **Berlin Winter Garden**, for example, one hundred-and-ten feet of thread was used.]

Fifth— Drinking the glass of water made no difference to the trick's function. It merely accented the "fact" that the needles and thread had indeed been swallowed. [Today, instructions to the trick suggest drinking a small glass of water for emphasis.]

And sixth— The bell sounding off-stage added drama to the overall effect.

In 1846, Robert-Houdin offered showmanship even Houdini lacked:

Louis-Philippe, king of France, had commanded the great magician to perform for his party at **Chateau St. Cloud**.

Robert-Houdin obliged by vanishing six silken handkerchiefs, giving his king the choice of three places for them to reappear. A vase on the mantelpiece in **Chateau St. Cloud**, a

The Magician's Fight!

nook beneath the **Hôtel des Invalides**, containing the tomb of Emperor Napoléon I. Or at the root of an orange tree in the conservatory.

The wily king mulled the choices over in his mind and decided to go with the orange tree, as the vase was too easy for the trickery he was watching and the **Hôtel des Invalides** too far to travel on such a hot day.

A footman was ordered to secure a spade and the royal party adjourned to the gardens where, beneath an orange tree, entangled in one of its roots was found a rusted iron box containing the six borrowed handkerchiefs.

Fastened to the handkerchiefs was an aged parchment, inscribed in faded ink:

> *This day, 6 June, 1786*
> *This iron box, containing six handkerchiefs, was placed among the roots of an orange tree by me, Balsalmo, Count de Cagliostro, to serve in performing an act of magic, which will be executed on the same day sixty years hence, before Louis of Orléans and his royal family.*

That is showmanship! The trick itself is good, but a crumbling parchment written by the hand of Cagliostro made it a masterpiece in sorcery. To think magic strong enough to traverse sixty years sent chills through the royal party.

Robert-Houdin could have simply vanished the borrowed handkerchiefs and reproduced them at a chosen location, and been considered a good magician. However, by antiquing a message from a magician long dead, he assured his fame forevermore.

James Charles Bouffard, Psy.D., Ph.D.

In 1895, Alexander Herrmann executed a delightful bit of deviltry, combining Robert-Houdin's miracle of 1846 with his own quality of showmanship:

Herrmann borrows a hat from a gentleman in the audience. He wraps this in a large handkerchief, places it on one of the tables, and covers it with a cone.

He then announces that he will cause the hat to disappear and turn up in the theater, the Town Hall, or any location in the town requested. And, to avoid any dispute, chance alone will decide where it is to be found.

Several spectators are each handed a slip of paper and asked to write a destination. All the notes are then folded and collected in a little bag. Further, to prevent any thought of collusion, a child is allowed to draw one of these slips from the bag.

Carriages are readied to take a committee in search of the soon to be vanished hat; to the place named on the paper chosen by the child.

Herrmann returns to the table, shows the hat once more, then wraps it a second time and covers it as before.

Taking his wand, he raps on the cone and commands it to go the place selected. The Town Hall!

The cone covering the hat is lifted. But nothing is gone! The package is still there. The assemblage begins to murmur and, as Herrmann appears undecided as to what to do, the mutterings increase. Evidently, Herrmann the Great has failed his trick.

He acts awkwardly, and completely confused. The audience begins to laugh at his embarrassment. Some applauding, some hissing.

Herrmann finally steps forward, stretches out his arms for silence, and asks in what way he has displeased his audience.

Someone suggests he put the question to the package on the table.

"Why?" asks Herrmann.

"To reproach it," replies one of his spectators, "for still being there."

"But it is in nobody's way."

"Well, did you not promise to send it on its way to the place written on the paper?"

"Yes, when I announced this, I said I would make the hat disappear. But I did not say that I would do the same for the handkerchief around it."

Herrmann grasps the handkerchief and shakes it to show it empty.

The hat has, indeed, gone on its way as promised.

The audience cheers approval and a committee is appointed to retrieve the hat, where it is found in the Town Hall sitting with regal authority atop the desk usually engaged by the head of the Town Council.

Although Alexander Herrmann was celebrated long before this effect, it must be noted that this captivating piece of showmanship helped establish him among the immortals in the art of magic.

A Case for Practice

Practice is the key to perfection in any endeavor.

As I write this, an anecdote comes to mind:

Some years ago, comedian Jack Benny was asked by host Johnny Carson of the **Tonight Show** if he ever practiced his violin.

"Whenever I can, on the road," answered Benny quite seriosly.

"Has it improved your playing?" inquired Carson.

"No!" quipped Benny... "But you have to practice even to be lousy, you know!"

Jack Benny was an excellent violinist. Had he chosen music as a profession — his mother's wish — he would have been among the best. Instead, he chose comedy, delivering laughter to millions through the precise instrument he practiced so diligently.

As with Jack Benny's violin, magic — as an entertainment value — must be practiced.

Whether you intend to go no further than the effects given in this work, or continue on to higher achievements in the art, remember to practice before presenting even the simplest sleight for a spectator.

Every successful magician, be they amateur, semi-professional or professional, has spent a considerable amount of time studying their reflection in a full-length mirror and addressing an imaginary audience.

For More on practice, see the **& Secrets** section.

A Note on Secrets:

Never reveal secrets to tricks based in this work, nor for varied tricks you may acquire in the future, to anyone

The Magician's Fight!

not truly interested in the profession. This is very important! Once the secret is out, the illusion is gone! You have not only spoiled it for others, but for yourself as well!

When Harry Houdini first met Beatrice Rahner he revealed his secrets to her, as his future assistant, with a solemn oath to never disclose them to anyone. And she never did!

One of the best answers to the query "How did you do that?" is a smiling, "I have no idea. I never could figure that one out."

For more on secrets, see the **& Secrets** section,

James Charles Bouffard, Psy.D., Ph.D.

"… magicians and poets, unlike philosophers, technicians, and sages, draw their powers from themselves…"
Octavio Paz
Mexican poet
(1914 – 1998)

& Secrets

Magician's Secrets!

Welcome to the wonderfully entertaining world of magic. You are about to enter a truly mysterious and fascinating realm of harmless deception. Or wizardry, if you will...

To begin, all feats of magic consist of:
1. **Effect.** What is seen by the spectator(s). Or the miracle brought about by you, the magician.
2. **Secrets and Preparation.** Secret to a trick and props needed.
3. **Method.** The technique used to present tricks to spectator(s).

Since the secret to a good magic trick is quite simple, don't judge it by this. Rather look to its effect on your audience.

Therefore, to secure a fascinating and memorable effect it is suggested you follow the below rules whenever you perform:

1. **Practice Before a Performance.** To enhance your performance, take time to rehearse. Whether you perform one trick for one or two spectators, or several in front a medium to large assembly, rehearsing [practicing] will increase your self-confidence more than you may ever imagine.
2. **Never Repeat a Trick.** The same effect done more than once for the same audience [or spectator] is likely to have the secret "uncovered." Your onlookers will know what to expect the second time around. Keep them surprised!
3. **Never Reveal the Secret.** When you expose the secret of a trick to non-magicians the magic, the mystery, the excitement, along with its entertainment value is lost. The fun, for all its intent and purpose, is gone!

Before propelling ourselves through the enlightened pages ahead, though, this author craves one more indulgence from his reader. **The Magician's Oath!** Once agreed upon, he or she may consider the world of magic officially theirs:

The Magician's Oath
As a magician I promise to never reveal the secret of an illusion to a non-magician without swearing them to the Magician's Oath. I promise never to perform any illusion, for any non-magician, without first practicing the effect until I can perform it well enough to maintain the illusion of magic.

Check here _ if you agree to the oath.
Or here _ if you disagree.

If you agree, then let's get started. The magic has been categorized for your convenience. Just decide on a selection of interest and have fun.

If you disagree, there is really not much we can do about that determination. Still, please be advised you may discover difficulty in following the instructions given. This is not an esoteric curse, but simply a psychological block. Our mind invariably does what our heart believes.

Card Magic:

Reverse Discovery

Effect:
This author believes one of the most baffling card effects is when the magician causes a selected card to reverse itself and appear face-up among a deck of face-down cards.

Secret and Preparation:
Simplicity is the cornerstone to this piece of magic. The trick depends upon the bottom card's reversal in the deck.

This is easily accomplished after the spectator has selected a card from the deck.

Here is how you would do it: Place the deck behind your back. Turn the bottom card face-up. Then turn the whole pack over so that all is face-up, except for the **face-down card on top**. While doing this, announce that: "After the selected card is memorized and replaced in the deck I am going to place the deck behind my back, as I am demonstrating, and locate it in the most startling manner."

Bring the deck out from behind your back. You are now ready for the spectator to replace the chosen card in the pack.

Method:

Spread the cards in your hands face-down in order for a spectator to freely select any card from the deck. [No **force** necessary.]

As soon as the card is selected, square up the deck and tell the spectator to look at and remember her card. Meanwhile, make the announcement described above, place the deck behind your back, and reverse the bottom card [as in **Secret and Preparation**].

While the spectator is focused on her card, or is showing her card to other spectators, bring out the deck from behind your back. The deck should be **face-up**, with the exception of the **face-down card on top**. Because of this single reversed card it appears the entire deck is face-down. [Take care to keep the deck squared so as not to "flash" the face-up pack below the single reversed top card.]

Hold the deck out firmly to the spectator in either your right or left hand [whichever is convenient for you]. Ask the spectator to push [or slip] in her card anywhere in the deck. Of course, unknown to the spectator, the card is really replaced into a face-up deck, **except for the face-down top card**.

When the spectator has inserted her card into the deck, put the deck behind your back. Then simply turn over [by touch] the single reversed top card and replace it face-up on the deck. Turn over the deck, square it up, then bring it out face-

The Magician's Fight!

down from behind your back. Every card in the deck, **except for the spectator's card**, is now facing in the same direction.

Explain that: "Since my spectator [or address the spectator by name] touched only one card in the deck, the chosen card was a bit warmer than the other cards." Further explain that: "Due to my highly developed sense of touch, I was able to find the card."

Hand the deck face-down to the spectator, step back with your palms toward her [to prove them empty], and tell her to spread out the cards from hand-to-hand or upon a table.

As the cards are spread, a startling thing happens. Only one card is seen face-up. The spectator's chosen one!

Tips:
1. With this method, you can perform this trick at any time. You may even allow the spectator to shuffle the deck before freely choosing a card.
2. When you first place the deck behind your back, do it naturally — as if you were just showing the spectator what is going to happen next.
3. When you do the "demonstration," **do not** tell the spectator her card will later be found face-up in a faced-down pack or you may alert her to the secret.

Fantastic Five

Effect:
A card is freely chosen by a spectator and replaced on top

of the deck. The pack is then given a cut. You spread the pack on the table, revealing that one card is face-up. It happens to be the Five of Hearts. You explain that the face-up Five of Hearts will serve as your magical indicator card. You then count down five cards in the spread deck, below the face-up card. Turning up the fifth card, it proves to be the card selected by the spectator. Now, if that were not enough, you turn over the four cards between the face-up Five of Hearts and the selected card. All four are Aces.

Secret and Preparation:

To prepare, run through the pack and remove the four Aces and the Five of Hearts. Square up the pack and place the Five of Hearts face-up on the bottom of the face-down pack. Place the four Aces face-down below the Five of Hearts. Square up the pack and you are ready to begin.

Method:

Fan the deck face-down [see **A Magical Glossary** for an explanation of the "fan"] and invite a spectator to choose a card. [No **force** necessary.] Be sure not to fan the pack too close to the bottom or you may risk accidentally exposing the face-up Five of Hearts.

Tell the spectator to remember her card. You then square up the deck and place it on a table.

Ask the spectator to put her card on top of the deck.

Cut the deck from left to right. Show your hands empty, then complete the cut by placing the bottom portion of the deck onto the top. [When the cut has been completed, the four Aces and the face-up Five of Hearts are placed directly above the selected card. Practice will help you perceive this.]

The Magician's Fight!

Spread the deck face-down on the table.

Call attention to the face-up Five of Hearts, then slide all the cards to its right.

"The face-up card is my magical indicator," you explain to your spectator. "It will help me locate your card. And, since the card is a five, that must be a clue."

Count five cards to the left of your indicator card, stopping on the fifth card.

Push the Five of Hearts and the four face-down Aces to the left of it.

Turn up the fifth card and show it to be the spectator's chosen card.

Now wait! Here the spectator will suppose the trick over. Not so! You turn over the four remaining cards to reveal the **Four Aces!**

[The appearance of the four Aces adds to this effect. It also is a great lead-in for any **Four Ace** trick you may know or wish to learn in the future.]

Money Magic:

Coin Through Leg

Effect:
You magically cause a coin to pass through your leg.

Secret and Preparation:
No preparation needed. The only requirement is an unprepared quarter or half-dollar and mastery of the **Finger-Palm**.

James Charles Bouffard, Psy.D., Ph.D.

[See **A Magical Glossary** for an explanation of the **Finger-Palm**.]

Display a coin to your spectator(s). The coin is held between the thumb and fingers of your right hand. [Or whichever hand is most convenient. If you are left-handed, reverse all instructions calling for use of the right hand or side.] Lower the coin to your right side, next to your right pants leg, just above the knee.

Place the coin on your leg, with your right hand pressing it there. Your right thumb holds the coin against your pants leg, just above the knee.

Bring your left hand over beside the coin. With the fingers of both your right and left hand, lift a portion of the pants fabric up and **under** the coin.

Fold the cloth, which you pulled under the coin, **up and over the coin**. Your left hand holds the fold of cloth in place. The coin will look completely covered to your audience, but practice will reveal it to be open and free of the pants fabric fold nearest the leg.

As soon as the coin is covered by the fold in the pants leg, the thumb of your right hand secretly pulls the coin **up and behind your right fingers.**

Finger-Palm the coin in your right hand, then move your right hand away and — slowly and deliberately — place it behind your left leg. [**Note: Your right hand will appear empty, while your left apparently still holds the coin behind the fold of cloth in your pants leg.**]

Here is the vanish: The left hand releases the fold of cloth in the pants leg. The fabric will drop, revealing the coin to have vanished. Turn your left hand over to show it empty.

And here is the coin through your leg: With your right

hand, slowly withdraw the coin from behind your right knee. The coin has magically gone through your leg.

Tips:
1. With this method you can perform **Coin Through Leg** at any time. You may even allow the spectator to examine the coin before and after the trick.
2. Use this as a clever sleight for any coin vanish routine, or as a sole effect described above. It is strongly suggested, however, that you either present it as a **vanish** or **coin through leg**. Not both as a single routine.

Dollars From Nowhere

Effect:
You show your hands front and backs. Then, bringing them together, a quantity of one-dollar bills appear from out of your empty palms.

Secret and Preparation:
First, a sport or suit coat is necessary to deliver this piece of magic properly.

Stack five or six one-dollar bills [larger bills may be used, should you wish]. Wind them into as tight a roll as you can. Place the roll of bills in the crook of your left elbow. Pull the fabric of your coat sleeve **up and over the roll**. Keep your arm slightly bent in order to hold the roll of bills in place.

You are now ready to face your audience.

Method:
With the roll of bills "loaded" as described above, reach over with your left hand and grasp your right coat sleeve at the crook of your elbow. Pull the sleeve back, clear of your right wrist, as you show your right hand empty.

Reach across with your right hand and grasp your left coat sleeve at the crook of your elbow, pulling that sleeve back and clear of your left wrist, as you show your left hand empty. During this move, it is quite natural for your right fingers to secretly "steal" the concealed bills from the fold in your jacket sleeve. [See **A Magical Glossary** for explanations of the "load" and "steal."]

The roll is held in your right hand between your fingers and palm. [Practice will help you with this.]

Bring both of your hands slowly together in front of you at shoulder-height, with your left hand in front of your right. This position will give you greater coverage for the next move.

Using the thumb and fingers of both hands, unroll the bills so they begin to appear at the top of your fingers.

After unrolling the bills halfway, suddenly pull your left hand down, so the thumb of your left hand unrolls the bills entirely from the bottom, leaving the open bills in your right hand. Fan the bills and display them to your baffled spectators. [Again, practice will clear this up nicely.]

Mental Magic:

When performing mental magic, strive to design an effect

The Magician's Fight!

in the **minds** of your audience as opposed to displaying your skills significantly as a master magician. Method, in this respect, is secondary and needs playing down to an extent no one should suspect trickery.

Magazine Test

Effect:

You present a sealed manila envelope and the current issue of a well-known magazine to your audience.

You explain that, prior to making your appearance, you wrote one word on a white card and sealed it in the envelope.

You hand the envelope to one of your spectators, then ask a second spectator to join you on the stage in an effort to demonstrate your ability as a mental magician.

You hand the magazine to this second spectator, together with a black felt-tip pen, request she place the magazine behind her back, open it and mark a bold **X** on any page at random with the pen. Then close it.

This done, you take back the magazine and invite the first spectator to open the envelope he was provided at the beginning of the experiment, and read the predicted word.

The magazine is spread to the marked page.

The second spectator calls out the word.

The audience is stunned to see the intersecting lines of the **X** go directly through the predicted word...

Secret and Preparation:

Use the current issue of a well-known magazine. Turn to any right-hand page located near the magazine's center and draw a large **X** on the page with a black felt-tip pen. Make sure the lines of the **X** cross over a single word. You may use any word as the "force" word [see **A Magical Glossary**].

Print the "force" word across the face of a white card and seal the "prediction" in a #10 manila envelope.

Finally, prepare a black felt-tip pen to prevent the spectator from actually making a mark on the magazine. [Leave the pen uncapped until the tip dries out.] Be sure this pen matches the one you used to mark the page.

Method:

Show the sealed envelope with the force word written on the card inside. Have a member of the audience hold the envelope.

Pick up a magazine and demonstrate how you would like a second spectator to mark the magazine page. Tell this spectator to thumb through the magazine while retaining it behind her back.

Once the spectator has selected a page, show her how to fold the left-hand pages to the rear. This will ensure the spectator "marks" on a **right-hand** page of the magazine. [Practice will clarify these and the following instructions.]

When you are sure the spectator understands the proper procedure for marking the magazine page, hand her the **prepared** pen. Ask the spectator to hold the magazine behind her back, select any **right-hand** page, fold the other [left-hand] pages out of the way, and mark the [right-hand] page with a large **X**. The prepared pen will insure no mark is actually made.

Have the spectator close the magazine before bringing it out from behind her back.

Take the pen and magazine from the spectator. Put the

The Magician's Fight!

pen away in your pocket. It has done its job.

Now call attention to the envelope held by the first spectator. Stress that the envelope was given to this spectator **before** the magazine had been marked! Have the spectator tear the envelope open and read aloud the word written on the card inside.

Give the magazine back to the second spectator and have her look through the pages until the marked sheet is located. When found, have her call out the word beneath the **X**.

Both the marked word and the word predicted on the card are **identical**!

Tips:
1. In rehearsal, do not use the magazine you intend for the test.
2. Practice marking the magazine page behind your own back before performing this trick. In fact, go through several trials to see how a pair of crossed lines would look when a spectator goes through the same process.
3. Then, when ready, pick up the magazine you intend to use for the test and copy your best previous attempt.
4. Giving the lines an irregular appearance will attach authenticity to the effect of this test.
5. Never let the **X** lines cross directly over the **center** of the word in the magazine. Rather aim near one end, or just above or below, yet close enough for everyone to agree on that word.

Impromptu Magic:

The purpose of impromptu magic, though appearing trivial and foolish at times, is to arouse interest in people who watch you perform. Once you earn their full attention, you will have acquired a receptive audience, which will — in turn — give you the self-confidence to launch a significant routine.

Magic Pulse Match

Effect:
During a casual conversation with friends [or even a demonstration for a small group of spectators], you proclaim to have discovered a magical way of checking your own pulse. You remove two plain wooden kitchen matches from your pocket and place one across the palm of your left hand. "This match," you explain, "will serve as the 'counter'." The second match is slipped under the first [match]. "This match," you say, "will serve as the 'transmitter'." As your spectators watch the counter, it is seen to rhythmically bounce — as if counting your heartbeats. Suddenly it stops, then starts beating erratically, bringing to a humorous end this cute little bit of magic. A spectator is handed the matches for examination, and offered a chance to duplicate the test.

Of course, he can't. And hands it off for another to try…

Secret and Preparation:
Use large wooden kitchen matches[available in any supermarket], for the best effect.

They are completely unprepared.

The secret to this experiment lies in your ability to manip-

The Magician's Fight!

ulate the "transmitter" match unseen.

Method:

Place the first match [the counter] across the palm of your left hand, the match-end resting against the side of your first finger, the match head pointed toward your little finger.

The second [transmitter] match is held between the thumb and first finger of your right hand, the match head pointed toward your little finger, your palm facing upward, your fingers bent into a loose fist **beneath** the matchstick. Your second finger presses its nail against the back of the matchstick [Practice will clarify this.].

When exerting pressure against the matchstick by the nail of your second finger, while slowly and imperceptibly sliding the matchstick across the nail, the match will create the necessary unseen pulsation.

Place your right and left hands together, positioning the "transmitter" match **under** the "counter" match. Secretly slide your right second fingernail across the [transmitter] match as described in the above paragraph. The right-hand transmitter will cause the left-hand counter match to jump in rhythmic beats.

Tips:

1. This is an excellent impromptu pocket trick if done well. Please do not attempt it without sufficient practice.
2. Remember, the "counter" match will not jump unless your right second fingernail is pressed firmly against the "transmitter" match as you slide it across [the nail].

James Charles Bouffard, Psy.D., Ph.D.

"Psychic" Magic:

The "Psychic" Bending of a Key

Individuals claiming genuine psychokinesis or telekinesis have fleeced the credulous and unwary for centuries.

These "psychic" prodigies have been both praised and condemned by news media throughout the years. Should they admit themselves showmen and sleight of hand artists, rather than alleging true powers of supernatural control, the media would no longer find room for condemnation and perhaps list them among our great magicians.

The following is a method for bending an ordinary house key using "psychic powers," as demonstrated in more recent history by persons asserting Extrasensory Perception [ESP]:

Effect:

An ordinary house key is handed to the audience for inspection, then returned.

The performer holds the key between his thumbs and first two fingers of both hands. With a deep, gazing concentration, he begins to rub the key and bend it up and down. Suddenly, a now bowed key is given to a member of his audience, who holds it aloft for all to see.

Secret and Preparation:

Two identical keys are used. Place one key in a vise and apply pressure to its free half with a pair of pliers until it bends. [A piece of cloth between the pliers and key will pre-

The Magician's Fight!

vent scratching.] Put both keys in a right-hand coat pocket, and you are ready.

Method:

The performer reaches into his right coat pocket and pulls out an unbent house key, **Finger-Palming** its bent twin, and passes it around for examination.

Upon retrieving the key, he grasps each end between the thumbs and first two fingers of both hands. [**Hold the key loosely between the tips of your thumbs and fingers.**] He rubs the key and bends his fingers up and down; giving the impression the key is bending.

Going through the bending motion long enough to establish this sensation, he then brings his thumbs and first fingers together—sliding them along the key until its surface is completely hidden [by his fingers]. This is where the "switch' is made. [**The unbent key is pushed into the left hand and held in place by the left thumb. At the same time, the bent key is slid into position between the hands. With practice, this movement works quite smoothly.** See **A Magical Glossary** for an explanation of the "switch."]

The left hand immediately drops to the performer's side, as his right offers the bent key to a member of his audience for inspection. [**While the bent key is handed to the spectator, your left hand drops the unbent key into a left-side pocket.** Note: If you are left-handed, reverse the foregoing maneuvers.]

Remember to use misdirection [see **A Magical Glossary**] to its utmost advantage in this trick. And showmanship is a must!

Another effect, averred authentic by professed psychics for decades, was witnessed on the old *You Asked For It!* TV series of the 1950s. Showmanship played a major role in this presentation and brought several million viewers literally to their knees. Until they realized the truth some years later.

As a trick, there is hardly any better. But do it as a trick, not as absolute proof of supernatural powers. Allow yourself the reputation of an expert mental magician. **Don't subject your character to disgrace as a fraudulent psychic...**

X-Ray Vision

In the not too distant past, this effect was accomplished by "seeing down the sides of the nose." A decidedly awkward and uncomfortable procedure.

Today, the following method is used most often:

Effect:

The performer's eyes are completely sealed by two pads of dough pressed into them, two half-dollars pressed into the dough, and two pads of cotton placed over all. Adhesive tape is applied to secure the pads to the performer's face.

Yet, subsequent to this extensive blindfolding, the performer is able to pour a glass of water from a pitcher without spilling a drop, name an object held by one of his spectators, and walk about as if his vision were not impaired in the least.

Secret and Preparation:

The secret is wrapped in its preparation.

You will need:

    1. Two small pads of soft dough. [Any kind of ready-

The Magician's Fight!

made bread or biscuit dough will do fine.]
2. Two half-dollar pieces. [Any bank can supply them.]
3. Two pads of absorbent cotton, about 2" x 3" in size. [These can be purchased from any drug store.]
4. A roll of hospital adhesive tape, 1/2" in width. [Also found in any drug store and most supermarkets.]
5. A pair of scissors.

Method:

As with any blindfold routine, this method will require a little time for the proper "touch." Have a trusted associate work with you long enough to gain that needed feel before presenting this deed...

The performer puts a pad of soft dough over his [closed] left eye, presses a half-dollar against the dough, and puts a pad of cotton over this. [**The 2" width of cotton is just above the eyebrow. The 3" length extends down over the eye to the bony structure beneath it.**] He holds the pad in place while a member of the audience slaps an "X" of two strips of tape over it. The "X" ends stick to the skin above and below the eye. [**While holding the pad in place for the spectator to fasten it down with tape, open your left eye and move the covering slightly so that a "gap" is made at the inner part of your eye — next to your nose. The gap does not have to be large to allow for clear vision. Practice should help you to understand this.**]

The right eye is covered in the same manner. [**This covering is "gapped" as with your left eye.**]

Next, the performer has the spectator apply a long strip of tape across his forehead, covering the top of both cotton pads.

Another tape is applied to the bottom of both pads, going straight across to under his ears. The spectator is cautioned to press these tapes firmly to his head. "The tighter these tapes are," says the performer, "the greater will be my incapacity to see." [**Yet, it is the very tightness of the *bottom* strip that will aid you in the trick's ultimate success. The tighter the *bottom* strip is applied, the wider the "gaps" in the pads will become. While pressing on the top tape, your thumbs — under cover of your fingers — can get you the needed openings. If you don't have ample vision when the taping is completed, don't worry. Simply — and boldly — pat and press on the pads and tapes, calling attention to the fact that you are now thoroughly blindfolded. Practice will make this clear.**]

The performer, completely blindfolded, proceeds to pour water from a pitcher into a glass, etc...

Some so-called psychics further shroud their vision with a cloth blindfold [or hood] in an effort to additionally dramatize this effect. They use a trick "see-through" blindfold [available from any magic dealer] for this. However, these blindfolds often fail rigid inspection and should be avoided. The blindfolding method as described is sufficient to accord you the reputation you seek.

A
Magical Glossary

"I'm not a magician. My avocation is magic. My vocation is director and actor. It takes a lot of talent and practice to be a magician. I did all the illusions on the show under the coaching of Mark Wilson. I was a catalyst for the magic of Mark [Wilson] and Larry Anderson. They deserve the applause."

Bill Bixby
Actor, Director
(1934 – 1993)
Reflecting on *The Magician* TV series.

A Magical Glossary

A

Acquitment: An unconvincing sleight for displaying both hands empty while concealing a small object [such as a coin].

Amateur magician: One who performs magic as a hobby. Many amateurs surpass the average professionals in skill, showmanship and overall presentation.

Among the most famous amateur magicians [who had occasionally displayed their ability for pay] include authors Charles Dickens and Lewis Carroll [*Alice in Wonderland*], ventriloquist Edgar Bergen. Actors Chester Morris, Orson Wells, James [Jimmy] Stewart, Hugh O'Brien [of TV's *Wyatt Earp*]. **Tonight Show** host Johnny Carson. And the great silent movie comedian Harold Lloyd.

Angle: The point of view the audience has when

watching a magician. You need be aware of audience angles when performing certain tricks. Otherwise, you risk revealing the secret.

Angle-proof: A device or effect, which allows for an audience view on all sides. [Such as in close-up magic.]

Apparatus: Articles specifically faked for a performance, as opposed to ordinary items used by a magician.

Appearance: A magical effect in which an object or person materializes.

Assistant: Someone who aids a magician during a routine or act. Usually part of his/her entourage. [Also see **Volunteer**.]

Audience: One or more persons whose attention has been brought successfully to the area of a performance.

B

Billet: In mental magic, a small piece of paper on which is written a message read by the magician without unfolding the paper for a look at its contents.

Billiard balls [magic]: Small balls, usually made of wood or plastic, used in manipulative magic.

C

Children's shows: Children are the most appreciative, yet most critical of spectators. Therefore, magicians must be sure of their ability before attempting a children's show. Any insecurity on the part of a performer will find itself detected sooner by a child than an adult.

Close-up magic: Shows availing small objects and sleight of hand. Usually for the amusement of a few spectators. Often the magician is standing behind or seated at a table during the performance.

Confederate [magic]: A secret assistant employed by a magician — usually posing as an audience volunteer — who aids in the successful completion of a trick.

Some magicians frown on the use of confederates as unethical. However, from an entertainment standpoint, confederates should not be dismissed. Many prominent magicians still rely on these "employed volunteers" to add much to a desired effect. An effect, which would have been lost without their use. [See **Volunteer**.]

Conjuring [new term]: The act of performing "miracles" through manipulative skills and specialized equipment. "Conjuring" and "magic" are synonymous. Therefore, a **magician** is a **conjuror**.

Conjuring [old term]:
The act of invoking demons to aid in producing miracles through supernatural means.

D

Dancing Handkerchief:
A parlor effect brought to the stage and assigned fame by Harry Blackstone, Sr.

Digtip:
A fake finger [or thumbtip], used to make silks or other small objects [coins, bills or sponges] appear or disappear.

Double-backed card:
Playing card with a back design on both sides.

Double-face card:
Playing card with a face design on both sides.

Double-lift:
A sleight enabling the magician to lift two or more cards from the top of a deck as if they were one.

E

Effect [magic]: A term referring to the apparent magic witnessed by an audience during, or at the completion of, a trick.

Escapologist: A magician who frees him/herself from restraining devices – including ropes, chains, jail cells. Harry Houdini is still our foremost escapologist.

F

Fake: A prop visibly ordinary to the audience yet gimmicked for the successful discharge of a magic trick or tricks.

Fan: Spreading playing cards in the hand to form a smart fan shape. [As in the oriental fan position.]

Finale: The final act or step in a routine. Usually a large and impressive finish.

Finger-Palm: Method for concealing a small object with the fingers while retaining the hand in a natural state.

Flap: A movable false bottom or top of a box, used

to hide a card.

Flash paper: A chemically treated [nitric acid] tissue paper that burst into flames instantly upon ignition. Used to vanish an article in a spectacular manner. [Usually a small object "wrapped" for the vanish.]

Force: Used to make a spectator pick a prearranged object, even though it is believed he/she has a free choice.

French drop: A sleight enabling the magician to retain a small object [a billiard ball, coin, thimble, etc.] in one hand, while spectators believe it has passed into the other.

G

Gimmick: A secret device used by a magician for the successful accomplishment of a trick. The "gimmick" should never be seen by the audience.

I

Illusion: Although any trick may be considered an illusion, this term is frequently ascribed to stage magic requiring large equipment.

L

Levitation: Effects that apparently defy gravity. [As in *The Floating Lady*, *Zombie Ball*, etc.]

Load [magic]: To introduce — secretly — an object before or during a trick. [Example: The rabbit is "loaded" into the hat during *The Rabbit in the Hat* trick.]

M

Magician's milk: An oily substance, when mixed with water resembles ordinary milk. [Used in *The Vanishing Milk* trick.]

Magician's wax: A pliable, putty-like adhesive used to attach a thread or an "invisible wire" to a small, light, object [usually a playing card] to cause it to "rise" or "float" in the air.

Marked deck: A deck of playing cards secretly coded to identify them without a need to look at the face.

Mental magic: A branch of magic which includes clairvoyance, telepathy and psychokinesis. All designed to baffle and amuse an audience without claiming supernatural powers.

Misdirection: A technique used to direct the audience's attention away from the secret movements of the magician. Sometimes this method diverts their unwelcome gaze from a concealed "gimmick."

O

Opener [magic]: The first effect, routine or act in a performance.

P

Palming [magic]: Concealment of a small object [card, coin, etc.] in the palm of your hand. Sometimes simply referred to as **Palm**.

Patter [magic]: An able technique employed by the magician to entertain — and often misdirect an audience — with stories, anecdotes, or just plain talk.

Penetration [magic]: An effect, whereby the magician establishes an illusion of one object passing through another without damage to either.

Prestidigitation: A sleight of hand term, interpreted as "nimble fingers" [also translated into "quick fingers"], phrased by French magician Jules de Rovere in 1815.

Production [magic]: To seemingly create something from nothing.

Professional magician: Performer who earns a living from the entertaining art of harmless magical deception.

R

Retention vanish: Sleight for vanishing a small object [coin, billiard ball, etc.] by transferring [tossing] it from one hand to the other.

This technique works due to the spectator's retina **retaining** the perceived image of an object for a fraction of a second after it is placed in the receiving hand — even though it is no longer there. [Note: If simple in its method, this vanish still needs thorough practice for the proper application of misdirection and showmanship.]

Routine: Well-rehearsed sequence of effects flowing into one another for an entertaining performance.

S

Semi-professional magician: Magical entertainer who performs for pay part-time.

Shell: Magic prop hollowed out and/or cut in half so the audience believes it a whole object [coins, blocks, wands, etc.].

Short card: A playing card about 1/16" shorter than others in the deck. [See **Svengali Deck**.]

Silent act: An act rendered in pantomime. The magician needs extreme manipulative skill for success in this type of performance.

Slack: Looseness in a rope or chain managed by the magician during an escape act.

Sleight: A skillful hand and/or finger move to secretly execute a desired portion of a magical effect.

Sleight of hand: The art of exhibiting magical effects through manual dexterity.

Steal [magic]: To **remove** an object secretly, as opposed to "load." [See **Load**.]

Stripper Deck: Deck of cards slightly shaved from one end to the other, allowing the magician to "strip" or pull out particular cards.

Sucker gag: Trick, which leads spectators to believe they have caught the magician in an embarrassing and confusing situation, only to end up embarrassed themselves.

Suspension: An effect, whereby a person or object floats in mid-air without a logical means of support. [See **Levitation**.]

Switch [magic]: Once called "ringing", the "switch" or "switching" is the secret substitution of a card or coin [or other object] to successfully complete a trick.

Svengali Deck: A deck of cards with alternating "short" cards of the same denomination and suit.
   First conceived by magician and mentalist Burling Hull in 1909, the idea was later stolen by medium W.D. LeRoy who would christen the deck for a fictitious evil hypnotist named Svengali. [Also see **Short card**.]

T

Talk [magic]: Telltale noise, as in the unskilled handling of multiple palmed coins or cards, which can ruin an otherwise effective manipulation. Apparatus will also "talk" if used improperly.

Thumb clip: A sleight used by the magician to secretly clip or hold an object between the base of the thumb and index finger.

Trick [magic]: An effect meant to fool an audience.

V

Vanish [magic]: A term purporting to cause an object or person to disappear.

Volunteer: An assistant chosen from the audience to aid a magician in a trick. Sometimes the "volunteer" is employed by the magician. [See **Confederate**.]

W

Well: A secret pocket in the magician's table.

Woofle dust: Imaginary powder with magical properties for help in vanishing small objects. [In his own act, this author would dissolve a knot to finish the **cut and restored rope** trick by sprinkling "woofle dust", claiming it "lint from my pocket." This was always good for a laugh. And would, effectively, allow a means for disposal of the actual knot.]

Miscellaneous

Courtesy: ©1999 A&L Magic, Inc.

"In a way, we are all magicians. We are alchemists, sorcerers and wizards. We are a strange bunch. But there is great fun in being a wizard."
Billy Joel
American singer and musician
(1949 –   )

Chapter Notes

Prologue:

1. Some records mark his place of birth as Dorchester, Oxfordshire County, England.
2. Although the Salem witch trials officially ended in 1692, the Reverends Increase and Cotton Mather tried for their reinstatement in order to "… lay waste to the impurities in our Godly society…" but failed in their attempts. Still, public burnings and hangings continued throughout the colonies, as well as both private and public executions persisting in other countries.

Chapter 1:

1. Also known as Khufu [2nd pharaoh (2589 – 2566), 4th Dynasty Egypt], accepted builder of the Great Pyramid of Giza.

2. From the Old Norse **Sloegâ**, meaning dexterity or deceptiveness [sleight]. **Sleight of hand** is often mistakenly written as **slight of hand.**
3. Frederick the Great banned Jacob Philadelphia from Potsdam when the latter read the former's mind during a royal engagement. Frederick was also adverse to Philadelphia's membership in the occult **Rosicrucian** order, which he had joined as a young man.

Chapter 2:

1. Some historians claim Torrini never lived, asserting no record has ever been found of him. Others believe the opposite. This author tends toward Torrini's existence. Whatever the decisive answer, however, the story constitutes good reading. And aims the young clockmaker in the right direction.
2. Some years later this theater was used by Georges Méliés (1861 – 1938), 19th and early 20th century stage magician and motion picture producer, as a backdrop for many of his pioneer films.
3. It is said a young newsboy named Tom Edison was so stimulated upon reading of Robert-Houdin's electrical experiments, he decided to try a few tests of his own.

Chapter 4:

1. The original Hungarian spelling was recorded as "Erik Weisz."

The Magician's Fight!

2. Jacob Hyman changed his name to Jack Hayman, joining vaudeville as a song-and-dance man.
3. Nickname of Theo "Houdini." Later known as "Hardeen."
4. The original monument was destroyed by vandals several times over the years and restored. In 1996, Houdini's defaced bust was finally repaired through funding arranged by magician David Copperfield.

Chapter 5:

1. From magician Harry Keller.
2. Harry's assistant during his U.S.O. war years.
3. Also called the **Haunted Handkerchief** and **Spirit Handkerchief**.
4. In 1927, Harry Blackstone co-founded the **Blackstone Magic Co.** with Percy Abbott, an Australian-born magician. Eighteen months later the two parted and Abbott took on a new partner, reopening as the **Abbott Magic Co.**
5. Arguably called "The Magic Capital of the World."

James Charles Bouffard, Psy.D., Ph.D.

"I think cinema, movies, and magic have always been closely associated. The very earliest people who made films were magicians."
Francis Ford Coppola
Director: **The Godfather**
(1939 –   )

Magical Trivia

Did You Know:

The **Royal Dynasty of Magic** originated when Alexander Herrmann's wand was passed to Harry Keller upon his death in 1896. Keller, in turn, passed the mantle [exemplified by a black cape] to Howard Thurston as he announced his retirement in 1908. Thurston extended the tradition by willing the mantle to Harry August Jansen [Dante the Magician] in 1936. Dante chose Lee Grabel to receive the mantle in 1955. Grabel retired in 1959, but waited until finding a suitable magician for the honor. On May 12, 1994, he presented the cape to Lance Burton ceremoniously at the Hacienda Hotel in Las Vegas, certifying him the newest member of the **Royal Dynasty of Magic** — representing magicians individually designated by a predecessor.

Hocus-pocus is an adulteration of the Latin prayer "Hoc ist corpus" [This is my body] used to consecrate the Roman Cattholic mass.

Numerable Catholic magicians — to this day — avoid use of the phrase.

In 1584, during the reign of Queen Elizabeth I, English justice Reginald Scot (ca 1538 – 1599) wrote *The Discoverie of Witchcraft*, holding that ..."prosecutions of those accused of witchcraft goes contrary to the dictates of reason and religion," placing responsibility expressly on the steps of the Roman Church. In 1603, all obtainable transcriptions were gathered and burned at the accession of James I — first in the Stuart line of British monarchs.

Although a Protestant, King James I never protested the intolerance permitted by Rome, fearing the engrafted Jesuit priests under Pope Clement VIII plotted a return of Catholic opposition to the magical arts in Great Britain — through his own death, if necessary.

Although pulling a rabbit from a hat is a classic symbol of magic, it has rarely been an integral part of a magic act.

Amusingly, the effect is said to have stemmed from the British public's fascination with the notorious case of Mary Toft, a Surrey housewife, who claimed giving birth to a litter of rabbits in 1726.

The Magician's Fight!

Magician John Nevil Maskelyne (1839 – 1917) held a patent on the pay toilet.

In Victorian 19th century he invented a unique lock for London toilets, which required a penny for operation. "Spend a penny" is a euphemism credited to this invention.

He would go on to acquire numerous patents, including the first typewriter manufactured in Britain.

Produced by the **Maskelyne British Typewriter & Manfacturing Co. Ltd.** of London in 1889, this ingenious typewriter featured a shift key enabled for operation by hand or foot [depending on the customer's preference] and a differential interspacing allowing each character to occupy space appropriate to printing width. A concept not introduced until 1941 with IBM's **Electromatic Model 04** electric typewriter.

Maskelyne's typewriter, as of this writing, is on display at **Science Museum**, South Kensington, London.

The oldest fraternal magic organization in the world is the **Society of American Magicians**, founded in the back room of Matinka's magic shop, New York City on May 10, 1902.

One of magician Howard Thurston's principal assistants, and the woman pictured in his **She Floats** levitation posters — Sadie Brady —, was the mother of comic actress Imogene Coca (1908 – 2001).

James Charles Bouffard, Psy.D., Ph.D.

Chung Ling Soo [William "Billy" Ellsworth Robinson, 1861–1918] was fatally shot while performing the dangerous **Bullet Catch** in 1918.

Rumors persisted for years after that his death was not accidentally caused by equipment malfunction, but the result of a jealousy-motivated murder.

Harry Houdini (1874–1926) was part owner and president of Matinka & Co. magic shop in 1919.

Houdini held a patent on an underwater diving suit, was a pioneer aviator and founded **Houdini Pictures Corporation**, in which he produced and starred in two films — *The Man From Beyond* [1921] and *Haldane of the Secret Service* [1923].

Though quitting the movie business, citing "lack of profits," in 1923, he received a star years later on the **Hollywood Walk of Fame** [7001 Hollywood Blvd.].

Dai Vernon [David F.W. Verner, 1894–1992], known as "The Professor," once accepted a bet to Houdini's boast that he could never be fooled by any trick he had seen performed at least three times in a row.

In Chicago, in 1919, Vernon stumped Houdini eight consecutive times with his version of **The Ambitious Card** effect. Each time, the master insisted Vernon "do it again." And, each time, Houdini shook his head in frustration. Final-

The Magician's Fight!

ly Bess, looking on anxiously, agreed with Vernon's friends when they chuckled, "Face it Houdini, you're fooled."

Some years later, Dai Vernon would tag a bill to his posters: "The Man Who Fooled Houdini."

Percy Thomas Tibbles (1881 – 1938) was the inventor of **Sawing Through A Woman**.

Although its conception debatably dates back to ancient Egypt, Tibbles — professionally billed as P.T. Selbit — is credited as the first modern magician to perform the illusion in January of 1921.

P.T. Selbit performing *Sawing Through A Woman* on a London stage, Jan. 1921.
Courtesy:
California Science Center
Exposition Park
700 State Drive
Los Angeles, CA 90037

The **Dancing [or Spirit] Handkerchief** was invented by Anna Fay [Born: Anna Norman, 1851–1927], a medium who used the handkerchief as a spirit apparition for her séances.

The Great Blackstone adapted the effect and added it to his own repertoire as an entertainment design.

In 1934, African-American magician Black Herman [Benjamin Rucker, 1892 – 1934], famous for a "buried alive" illusion, actually collapsed and died onstage.

His devoted fans would not believe he was dead and gathered outside a funeral home, where the body was on display for its final viewing, awaiting the trick's end.

"Perhaps we should charge admission," one of Herman's assistants finally piped. "That's what he would have done."

And so they did.

In 1957, Cardini [Richard Pitchford, 1895–1973] performed the only known taped footage of his act on **The Festival of Magic** TV show at the age of 62.

Cardini, named the "greatest exponent of pure sleight of hand the world has ever known" in 1958 by the **New England Magic Society**, would captivate audiences for years to come.

Magical Reading

You can borrow the following excellent books [some on DVD] from most public libraries. Or purchase from your favorite magic dealer.

Card Magic:

- ***Expert Card Technique: Close-Up Table Magic**/* Jean Huggard and Frederick Braue

- ***Self-Working Close-Up Card Magic**/* Karl Fulves

- ***Close-Up Magic**/* Harry Lorayne

- ***Card Manipulation**/* Jean Huggard

- ➢ ***Royal Road to Card Magic/*** Jean Huggard and Frederick Braue

- ➢ ***Scarne on Card Tricks/*** John Scarne

- ➢ ***Encyclopedia of Card Magic/*** Jean Huggard

- ➢ ***Magic by Blackstone***

- ➢ ***Card Magic for Amateurs and professionals/*** Bill Simon

Money Magic:

- ➢ ***Self-Working Coin Magic/*** Karl Fulves

- ➢ ***Modern Coin Magic/*** J.B. Bobo

- ➢ ***Money Magic/*** Jean Huggard

- ➢ ***Switch: Unfolding The $100 Bill Change/*** John Lovick

- ➢ ***Folding Money Fooling/*** Robert Neale

Mental Magic:

- ➢ ***Self-Working Mental Magic/*** Karl Fulves

The Magician's Fight!

- ***Annemann's Practical Mental Magic/*** Theodore Annemann

- ***Mind Magic/*** Marc Lemezma

- ***13 Steps to Mentalism/*** Corinda

Impromptu Magic:

- ***Impromptu Card Magic/*** compiled by Aldo Colombini

- ***Life Savers/*** Michael Weber

"Psychic" Magic:

- ***Psychokinetic Touches/*** Banachek [Steve Straw]

- ***Psychokinetic Time/*** Banachek [Steve Straw]

James Charles Bouffard, Psy.D., Ph.D.

"… as a conjuror, three things are essential — First, dexterity; Second, dexterity; and Third, dexterity."
Harry Keller
(1849 – 1922)

[Author's note: Although a foremost magician during his time, Harry Keller believed little in the grade of showmanship defined in this work.]

Bibliography

The below represents but a small portion of the books and papers studied during preparation for this work. Though the author has found some a matter for dispute, all of the writings were thoroughly examined and cross-referenced for as much an accurate analysis as is humanly possible.

Still, he feels sure any shortcomings on his part will find themselves redressed by future writers of the art.

Ankarloo, Bengt and Clark, Stuart (editors.). ***Witchcraft and Magic in Europe: The period of the Witch Trials***. University of Pennsylvania Press, Philadelphia, PA, 2002.

Baily, Michael D. ***Battling Demons: Witchcraft, Heresy, and Reforms in the Late Middle Ages (Magic in History)*** Pennsylvania State University, University Park, PA, 2003.

Baroja, Julio Caro. *The World of Witches*. Phoenix Press, New Haven, CT, 2001.

Bierce, Ambrose Gwinett. *The Devil's Dictionary*. Dover Publishing, 1971 edition [first pub., 1911].

Boyer, Paul and Nissanbaum, Stephan. *Salem Possessed: The Social Origins of Witchcraft*. Harvard University Press, Cambridge, MA, 1974.

Brier, Bob. *Ancient Egyption Magic*. Harper Paperback, 1998.

Cavendish, Richard. *The Black Arts: An Absorbing Account of Witchcraft, Demonology, Astrology, and Other Mystical Practices Throughout the Ages*. The Berkley Publishing Group, New York, NY, 1967.

Crow, W.B. *Witchcraft, Magic and Occultism: A Fascinating History*. Wilshire Book Co., No. Hollywood, CA, 1950.

Doerflinger, William. *The Magic Catalogue: A Guide to the Wonderful World of Magic*. E.P. Dutton, New York, 1977.

Flint, Valerie Irene Jane. *The Rise of Magic in Early Medieval Europe*. Princeton University Press, Princeton, NJ, 1994.

Godbeer, Richard. *The Devil's Dominion: Magic and Religion in Early New England*. Cambridge University Press, NY, 1994.

Griley, Rosemary Ellen. *The Encyclopedia of Witches and Witchcraft*. Facts on File, New York, 1989.

Hole, Christina. *Witchcraft in England*. Scribner's, New York, 1947.

Hurley, Aldous. *The Devils of London*. Harper & Bros., New York, 1952.

Kiechefer, Richard. *Magic in the Middle Ages*. Cambridge University Press, United Kingdom, 1989.

Kettridge, George Lyman. *Witchcraft in Old and New England*. Harvard University Press, Cambridge, MA, 1929.

Lawrence, Jeremy. *Innocent Persecutions*. Self-published, 1805.

Lea, H.C. *A History of the Inquisition of the Middle Ages*. London, 1906.

Levi, Eliphas. *The History of Magic: includ-*

ing a clear & precise exposition of it procedure, its rites & mysteries. Translated by A.C. Waite. Rider & Co., London, 1920.

Mather, Increase. *Cases of Conscience Concerning Evil Spirits*. Printed and sold by Benjamin Harris at the London Coffee House, 1693.

McFarland, A.D. *Witchcraft in Tudor and Stuart England*. Harper & Row, 1970.

Mesello, Robert. *Raising Hell: A Concise History of the Black Arts —and those who dared to Practice Them*. The Berkley Publishing Group, New York, NY, 1967.

Meyer, Marvin W. and Smith, Richard. *Ancient Christian Magic*. Princeton University Press, Princeton, NJ, 1999.

Peters, Edward. *The Magician, the Witch and the Law*. University of Pennsylvania Press, PA, 1978.

Seligmann, Kurt. *The History of Magic and the Occult*. Gramacy Books, New York, NY, 1997.

Theobald, J.D. *Magic and its Mysteries*. Frederick Warne, London, 1880.

The Magician's Fight!

Waite, Gary K. *Heresy, Magic and Witchcraft in Early Modern Europe (European Culture and Society)*. Palgrave MacMillan, Ltd., New York, NY, 2003.

Wehman, Henry. *Wizard's Manual*. [self-published] Wehman, New York, NY, 1895.

James Charles Bouffard, Psy.D., Ph.D.

"Whatever deceives seems to exercise a kind of magical enchantment."
Plato
(ca 428 B.C.E. – 347 B.C.E.)

Index

An italicized *n* following a page number is a chapter note.

A

Abbott Magic Co. 125*n*
Abbott, Percy. 125*n*
Acquitment. 109
Alexander III, Czar [Russia]. 35
Algeria [French North Africa]. 33
Ambitious Card, The. 130
Angle. 109-110
Angle-proof. 110
Apparatus. 110
Appleton [WI]. 44
Assistant. 110
Attila the Hun. 23
Audience. 110

B

Babylonia. Preface
Beck, Martin. 47
Belgium. 33
Benny, Jack. 84
Berlin Winter Garden. 80
Bey, Rahman. 48
Billet. 110
Billiard balls [magic]. 111
Blackstone, Jr., Harry. 54
Blackstone, Sr., Harry. 52, 55-56, 125*n*
Blackstone Magic Co. 125*n*
Blouse [France]. 33-34
Boston, George. 52
Boston [MA]. Preface
Bouton Brothers, The. 51
Bouton, Harry [Boughton, Henri]. 51
Bouton, Pete. 51
Bradford [PA]. 39
Bradstreet, Simon. 23
Brady, Sadie. 129
Britain, Great. 28, 128
Buffalo [NY]. 40
Bullet Catch. 31, 129
Burton, Lance. 127

C

California Science Center. 131

Index

Cardini. 132
Card Magic. 89-93
Carson, Johnny. 84
Cases of Conscience Concerning Evil Spirits. 22-23
Catherine II [Russia]. 29
Catholic. 128
Charles IX [king of France]. Preface
Chateau St. Cloud. 80
Chicago [IL]. 130
Children's shows. 111
Chocat, Piérŕe. 33
Christianity. 29
Chung Ling Soo [William Ellsworth Robinson]. 43, 129
Clement VIII, Pope. 128
Close-up Magic. 111
Coca, Imogene. 129
Coin Through Leg. 93-95
Colon (MI). 54
Coney Island. 47, 78
Confederate. 111, 120
Conjuring [new term]. 111
Conjuring [old term]. 112

Conjuror. 28-30, 31, 111
Copperfield, David. 125n
Cups and balls. 28
Cut and restored rope. 120

D

Dancing Handkerchief. 53, 112, 132
Dante [See Jansen. Harry August]
Dean of American Stage Illusionists, The. 52, 56
de Cagliostro, Count. 81
Dedi. 27
Ded-Snefru. 27
de Grisy, Count Edmond. 31
de Grisy, Giovanni. 31
Denver [Co]. 37
de Rovere, Jules. 116
Devil, The. 20, 28
Digtip. 112
Discoverie of Witchcraft, The. 128
Dollars From Nowhere. 95
Dorchester [England]. 123n

Index   145

Double-backed card. 112
Double-face card. 112
Double-lift. 112

E

East Indian Needle
   Mystery, The [Now
   called The Needle
   Trick]. 78-80
Edison, Tom. 124*n*
Effect [magic]. 113
Egypt. Preface, 27, 131
Egyptians. Preface
Electromatic Model 04
   Electric typewriter,
   IBM's. 129
Elizabeth I, Queen
   [England]. Preface, 128
Emile [Robert-Houdin's
   Son]. 32
England. Preface, 27, 33
Escapologist. 113
Eugene [Robert-Houdin's
   Son]. 32
Europe. 27-28, 36

F

Fake. 113

Fan. 92, 113
Fantastic Five. 91-93
Father of Lies, The. 20
Faust. 37
Fay, Anna. 132
Festival of Magic, The
   [TV show]. 132
Final Act, The. 54
Finale. 113
Finger-Palm. 93-94, 103,
   113
Flap. 113
Flash paper. 114
Floating Lady, The. 115
Force. 90, 92, 98, 114
Four Aces. 93
France. 33-34, 35
Franklin, Benjamin. 29
Frederick the Great [magician]. 52
Frederick the Great [Potsdam]. 29, 124*n*
French drop. 114
French North Africa. 33

G

Germany, 33, 76
Gimmick. 114
Goldin, Horace. 56

Index

Grabel, Lee. 127
Grant, Ulysses S. 38
Great Blackstone, The. 51, 54, 56, 132
Great Northern Theater. 42
Great Pyramid of Giza. 123*n*
Greece. Preface
Greeks. Preface

H

Hacienda Hotel [Las Vegas, NV]. 127
Haldane of the Secret Service. 130
Hamilton [See Chocat, Piérŕe]. 33
Hanover [Germany]. 35
Hardeen, Theo [Dash]. 43, 45, 125*n*
Haunted Handkerchief. 125*n*
Hayman, Jack. 125*n*
Henry VIII [king of England]. Preface
Herman, Black. 132
Herrmann, Adelaide. 38-39, 43

Herrmann, Alexander. 35-42, 55-56, 82-83, 127
Herrmann, Carl [Compars]. 35-35, 56
Herrmann, Leon. 41, 43
Herrmann the Great [See Herrmann, Alexander]
Hippodrome Theater. 77
Hocus-pocus. 47, 128
Hoffman, Professor Louis. 34
H. Richter's Sons Necktie Factory. 45-46
Hôtel des Invalides. 81
Houdin, Joséphine Cécile. 32
Houdini, Beatrice [Bess]. 43, 46-49, 79, 89, 130
"Houdini Brothers." 45-46
Houdini, Harry. 32, 43-50, 55, 76-80, 125*n*, 130-131
Hyman, Jacob. 45, 125*n* [Also see Hayman, Jack]

I

Illusion. 114
Impromptu Magic. 99-101

Index

Innocent Persecutions. 22-23
Inquisitions. 23
Ireland. 33
Isabella II, Queen [Spain]. 36

J

James I [king of Great Britain]. 128
Jansen, Harry August [Dante the Magician]. 127
Jesuit priests. 128

K

Katterfelto, Dr. Gustavus. 29-30, 55-56
Keller, Harry. 43, 125n, 127, 136
Kheops [pharaoh, ancient Egypt]. 27
Khufu [Also see Kheops]. 123n
Knickerbocker Hotel [Hollywood, CA]. 48

L

Lakeside Cemetery [MI]. 54
Lawrence, Jeremy. 22-23
Les Secrets de La Prestiditation et de La Magie. 33-34
Leverett, John. 23
Levitation. 114, 119, 129
Lincoln Theater [Decatur, IL]. 53
Little Treatise on Strange and Appropriate Feats. 29
Load [magic]. 96, 115
Lockman, Earle. Dedication, 22
Louis IX [king of France]. 28
Louis-Phillipe [king of France]. 80
Lyceum Theater [NY]. 39, 40, 41

M

Machpelah Cemetery [NY]. 48
Magazine Test. 97-99
Magical Glossary, A. 92, 93, 96, 98, 103

Index

"Magic Capital of the World, The" [Colon, MI]. 125*n*
Magician, Amateur. 109
Magician's Milk. 115
Magician's Oath, The. 88-89
Magician, Professional. 117
Magic Pulse Match. 100-101
Magician, Semi-professional. 117
Magician's Wax. 115
Man From Beyond, The. 130
Marked deck. 115
Maskelyne British Typewriter & Manufacturing Co. Ltd. [London]. 129
Maskelyne, John Nevil. 129
Matinka's magic shop. 129, 130
Méliés, Georges. 124*n*
Mental Magic. 96-99, 115
Metamorphosis. 47
Misdirection. 103, 115

"modern magic, the father of." 32
Money Magic. 93-96
"Mr. Show Business of the West." 47

N

Napoleon I, Emperor [France]. 81
Napoleon III, Emperor (France). 33
Needle Trick, The. 78-80
New England Magic Society. 132
New Tops, The [conjuror's magazine]. 56
New York City [NY]. 39, 41, 44, 77-78, 129
New York Times [newspaper]. 39-40
Norman, Anna [See Fay Anna]

O

Opener [magic]. 116
Orléans, Louis of. 81
Orpheum Vaudeville chain. 47

Index

P

Palais Royal. 32-33
Palming [magic]. 116
Paris [France]. 32-33, 35-36, 41
Patter [magic]. 116
Pay toilet. 129
Penetration [magic]. 116
Pennsylvania, 29
Philadelphia [PA]. 29, 77-78
Philadelphia, Jacob. 29-30, 55-56, 77, 124n
Pictures Corporation, Houdini [NY]. 130
Practice. 83-106
Prestidigitation. 116
Prince of Evil, The. 20
Production [magic]. 117
"Professor, The." 130
Protestant. 128
"Psychic" Bending of a Key, The. 102-103
"Psychic" Magic. 102-106

Q

R

Rabbit in the Hat, The. 115
Rahner, Wilhelmina Beatrice [See Houdini, Beatrice]
Rambo Drugstore [Decatur, IL]. 53
Retention Vanish. 117
Reverse Discovery. 89-90
Robert, Jean Eugene. 31 [Also see Robert-Houdin]
Robert-Houdin. 32-34, 35, 45, 46, 56, 80-82, 124n
Rochester [NY]. 39, 40, 42
Romans, Preface
Rome. Preface, 128
Rosicrucian [occult order]. 124n
Routine. 117
Rucker, Benjamin [See Herman, Black]
Rue Robert-Houdin. 34
Royal Dynasty of Magic. 127

Index

S

Salem. 20
Salem witch trials. Preface, 123*n*
Samuel [Herrmann]. 35
Satan. 20
Sawing a Woman [or Lady] in Half. 131
Sawing Through A Woman. 131
Scarcez, Adelaide [See Herrmann, Adelaide]
Science Museum [London]. 129
Scot, Reginald. 128
Scotland. 20, 33
Séance. 29, 48, 49, 132
Secrets. 84-106
Secrets of Conjuring and Magic. 34
Selbit, P.T. 131
She Floats. 129
Shell. 118
Showmanship. 55, 77-83, 103-104, 109, 111, 117
Slack. 118
Silent act. 118
Sleight. 118
Sleight of hand. 27, 45, 102, 118, 124*n*, 132
Sloegâ [Old Norse]. 124*n*
Society of American Magicians. 129
Soirées Fantastique. 32-33
Spain. 36
Spirit Handkerchief. 125*n*, 132
St. Gervais [France]. 34
St. Petersburg [Russia]. 35
State Industrial School [Rochester, NY[. 42
Star Theater [Brooklyn, NY]. 36
Steal [magic]. 96, 118
Stripper Deck. 118-119
Sucker gag. 119
Sultan Mustapha [Constantinople]. 29
Surrey [England]. 128
Suspension. 119
Svengali Deck. 119
Switch [magic]. 103, 119

T

Tabor Opera House [CO].

Index

37
Talk [magic]. 119
Terrible One, The. 20
Testament, Old. Preface
"The Brothers Houdini." 47, 48
"The King of Cards." 46
Thumb clip. 120
Thurston, Howard. 127, 129
Tibbles, Percy Thomas [See Selbit, P.T.]
Toft, Mary. 128
Tonight Show, The. 84
Torrini. 31, 124*n*
Trick [magic]. 120

U

Unmasking of Robert-Houdin, The. 32, 78

V

Vanishing Audience, The. 53
Vanishing Milk, The. 115
Vanish. 120

Verner, David F.W. [See Vernon, Dai]
Vernon, Dai. 130-131
Volunteer. 120

W

Walk of Fame, Hollywood. 130
Walnut Street Theater [PA]. 77
Warlock. 19
Weiss, Erich [See Houdini, Harry]
Weiss, Mayer Samuel [Houdini's father]. 44
Weisz, Erik [Erich's Hungarian spelling]. 124*n*
Well. 120
Witch. Preface, 19-23, 28
Witchcraft. Preface
Witch-hunt(s). Preface, 28
Woodlawn Cemetery [New York City]. 39
Woofle dust. 120

X

X-Ray Vision. 104-106

Y

You Asked For It! [1950s
  TV series]. 104

Z

Ziegfeld, Florenz. 48
Zombie Ball. 115

The Magician's Fight!

"The magic of drama is infinitely more powerful than the magic of trickery. It is as available to the conjurer as it is to the actor. The only difference is that actors take it for granted, whereas few conjurers are even aware that it exists."
Henning Cunningham Nelms
Magic and Showmanship
(1900 – 1986)

About the Author

Dr. Bouffard holds an LL.B. from LaSalle University, a Masters and Psy.D. from Neotarian College of Psychology. And has spent thirty years as a psychological counselor.

He's participated in various businesses, both as a partner and sole owner.

Besides historical research, his passionate love is magic as an art and entertainment. As Dr. Jimini, M.E. [Magical Entertainer], he's made numerous charitable and paid appearances.

In the middle 1960s, he was co-owner of a joke and magic store — *Alhambra Fun Shop* — in Alhambra, CA and partnered a tavern in West Covina, CA, where customers could enjoy "a quick drink, good company, and a little magic."

In 1999, he earned a Ph.D. (a candidacy shelved for over twenty years due to time restraints) in Theocentric Business and Ethics from American College of Metaphysical Theology, leading to ministerial credentials.

Currently, Dr. Bouffard is devoting much of his time to writing informational books, manuals, and managing a supportive Internet presence called *Doc Jim's Help Page!*

www.ingramcontent.com/pod-product-compliance
Lightning Source LLC
LaVergne TN
LVHW011422080426
835512LV00005B/207